NEPTUNE'S TABLE

NEPTUNE'S TABLE

Cooking The Seafood Exotics

Written and illustrated by

Don Hubbard

Sea Eagle Publications

Coronado, California

Sea Eagle

Publications

Previous books by the same author:

SHIPS-IN-BOTTLES: A Step-By-Step Guide to a Venerable Nautical Craft

The Complete Book of Inflatable Boats

Where to Kayak in San Diego County and Nearby Mexico

Published by Sea Eagle Publications

Post Office Box 180550,

Coronado, California 92178, USA

First Edition

Printed in Hong Kong

Library of Congress Cataloging-in-Publication Data

Hubbard, Don, 1926 -

Neptune's Table : cooking the seafood exotics / written and illustrated by Don Hubbard.

p. cm.

Includes Index.

ISBN 0-943665-06-X

1. Cookery (Seafood)   I. Title.

TX747.H87 1997

641.6'92--dc21   97-8475

                                                        CIP

To all those who enjoy the creatures of the sea both for their beauty and their flavor

ACKNOWLEDGMENTS

No worthwhile book can be completed without the help and support of others. The people who were involved with me in this book include my companion, Kay Frances Boldt, and my children Leslie, Christopher and Lauren who cheerfully slugged it though the many meals, some pretty unusual, that I produced over the years.

My good friends Dallas Boggs, Rick Ortenblad and Sue Fellows for their encouragement and suggestions while on our many Baja and ocean kayaking trips.

Janet Leo, Creela Martin-Villani, Katy Reeve Weesner, Ed Ray, Nathalie Martensen and Chris and Wendy Nair (the latter two from Jabalpur, India) for their recipe suggestions.

My sister, Doris, and my brother-in-law, Bill Hesse, who shared the 1930s High Island seafood catches with me and who reminded me of some of the exciting happenings in those early years.

Bette Overman, Elizabeth Lehner, Donna Bean and Ed Ray for the time they spent copy editing.

Good friends, Eric and Gretchen Boldt; Beverly Ady; Dottie and Haydn Huntley; Dr. Eric Skovenborg and Per Christensen in Denmark for their interest and encouragement.

Elly de Koster in Holland for her friendship and Dutch mussel recipes.

Jack Hinkley and Ray Handwerker, both of ship-in-bottle fame, for their enthusiasm for the project.

Sandy, Anna and the other ladies at Classic Reprographics for their help and advice concerning color reproductions.

Bill Johnson and the various crews on the Bottom Scratcher diving boat who led me to some of the finest seafood gathering spots along the California and Baja coasts.

And finally, the friendly personnel at the Coronado Public Library who were always helpful when I needed some obscure reference work.

CONTENTS

Disclaimer

The information contained in this book is intended for reference purposes only. The reader should be aware that certain seafoods may cause allergic reactions in some people and that some seafoods have high levels of cholesterol or sodium which may be incompatible with persons suffering from high blood pressure or who are on cholesterol lowering diets. General nutritional guidelines are provided in Appendix A, but they too are subject to variation due to conditions at the place where the catch was taken, such as water temperature and salinity, time of year and other conditions.

Consult with your physician if you have questions concerning the inclusion of seafood in your diet.

This book has been published with the express purpose of informing the reader about certain food combinations which the author has found appealing. The author and Sea Eagle Publications shall accept no liability or responsibility to any person or entity for loss or damage caused, or alleged to have been caused, directly or indirectly by the information contained in this book.

If you do not wish to be bound by the above please return this book to the bookstore where you purchased it for a full refund.

ILLUSTRATIONS

ABOUT THE AUTHOR

Don Hubbard is a retired Navy Commander who enjoys the blessings of both good health and curiosity about the world around him. Originally from the Bronx, New York, he entered the U.S. Navy in 1943 during World War II. He completed his qualifications as a naval aviator in 1947 and went on to serve in three squadrons and amass 4,000 hours of flight time in multi-engine attack and reconnaissance aircraft. He retired in Coronado, California, in 1967 upon completion of a one year tour of duty in Vietnam.

As a civilian Don was attracted to the excitement of the underwater world and established a large scuba diving school in San Diego (Ocean Ventures). He is a qualified scuba instructor certified by both the National Association of Underwater Instructors (NAUI #1422) and The Professional Association of Diving Instructors (PADI #1310). Over the years he has certified over 1000 students in both basic and advanced underwater activities.

His diving school extended to include diving tours into the prime waters surrounding Mexico's Baja peninsula where he began experimenting with inflatable boats because of their portability, stability and large carrying capacity. Exploiting his knowledge of these craft he opened a successful retail store which specialized in inflatables and paddle craft. Both the diving and boating businesses were sold in 1977 so that he could turn his attention to art (watercolor and gyotaku) and writing.

His first book, Ships-In-Bottles: A Step-By-Step Guide to a Venerable Nautical Craft was originally published by McGraw-Hill and then republished by his own company, Sea Eagle Publications in 1988. His second book, The Complete Book of Inflatable Boats, was published by Western Marine Enterprises in 1981. Both of the foregoing books are considered classics on the subjects concerned. Don has been a paddling enthusiast all his life and was one of the first to regularly use sea kayaks for ocean operations in the San Diego area. Using his accumulated knowledge he wrote and published his small book, Where To Paddle in San Diego and Nearby Mexico, which is now a standard paddling guide for the area. He has served on the Board of Directors of the 500 person San Diego Watercolor Society, The Coronado Art Association and The Ships-In- Bottles Association of America, which he founded in 1983. He has been a member of the Nature Printing Society since 1978.

During much of his Navy career, and all of the time since then, he has been engaged in experimenting with and cooking the endlessly varied and often unusual and exotic cuisine of the sea. His attraction to cookery as an art form led to the production of this current book.

Future books include The How-To Book of the Nautical Arts and Crafts; and GYOTAKU: The Art of Nature Printing. Both are nearing completion and should be available by late 1998.

PREFACE

Aside from being low calorie and low waste, one of the advantages of seafood, both the shell fish that I address and other types, is that it can be cooked very simply and rapidly and still be tasty and fulfilling. Admittedly, for convenience most of the sea food we prepare for ourselves falls into the simple category. On the other hand, seafood can be greatly enhanced by the addition of very few additional ingredients. The fun of producing a cookbook is the chance to experiment with these ingredients to produce new or refined versions of old recipes. This also dictates that the recipes be tested in your own kitchen with the attendant good smells and flavors. Many times I won at this game and sometimes I lost, but even the losers taught valuable lessons. A bit of wine, a few herbs, some butter, half-and-half or cream. These things can turn the produce of the sea into dishes that the Gods will favor and demand at Neptune's Table. Thus the name of this book. Hopefully, Neptune will agree with me and help you to transform some of the enclosed recipes into memorable feasts. For your part, please examine my cooking combinations and then have fun too. Alter them by adding or subtracting ingredients to suit your own personal taste. With these beginnings plus your own individual fingerprints, this book can be the start of a life-long seafood adventure.

Since World War II we have seen the migration of large numbers of Asians to our shores. These people have always had an affinity for seafood and in the areas they settle, they have established markets which cater to their tastes. I seek these out, and find there not only a wide variety of fresh seafood, but many frozen items with unique characteristics. Top snail meat, frozen cooked steamer clams and large frozen octopus are among the latter. In addition, the Asian markets feature condiments, such as fish sauce (noùc màm or Patis) and sweet/hot Thai chili Sauce which are not normally available on supermarket shelves. Check these stores out when you find them. They can add a lot of surprises to your cooking.

Good luck and good eating!

INTRODUCTION

I have been lucky enough to have had a life-long love affair with the sea. I grew up in the Bronx, in New York, but had the good fortune to spend my summers and part of the autumn on a small island (High Island) in Long Island Sound. This was truly an island, and in the earliest years there was not even a bridge across. We came and went by canoe or by walking across the sandbar at low tide. Later a foot bridge was built, but it was still more than a mile walk to the nearest market. For years there was no electricity and our light at night was a kerosene lamp. Our perishable food was stored in an ice box, and the ice, too, had to be hauled in.

Long Island Sound is about three miles wide where High Island is located and before World War II we could easily see the two and three masted schooners which used to haul stone and other commodities from New England to New York City. We spent about five months of the year on the island, from June through October. Our two-room bungalow was built by my dad and sat high on the rock facing almost directly northeast, which about parallels the direction of the Sound itself. We could see and hear the lighthouse on Execution Rocks a few miles away, and look across to the then large estates on the north shore of Long Island. Each Fall we would be treated to impressive storms, when the "Nor'easters" would come rolling in. With virtually nothing to divert them, the storm waves would grow in this unobstructed fetch until they were huge, and then fling themselves on the black sandstone rocks below our bungalow in a crashing, spraying mass.

Understandably, as a part of this oceanic existence, seafood became a permanent part of my life. The Sound was relatively free from pollution then and the take from the surrounding waters added much to our daily diet. Crabs, clams, lobsters and fish were abundant and learning the gathering skills was one of my pleasures.

The southwestern side of High Island had two collecting areas. There was a long sandbar that was exposed at low tide which joined High Island with its larger neighbor, City Island. This bar was a rich mine. There were pockets of tape worms and biting sand worms, which we collected to use as bait. There were also soft shelled "steamer clams" which we dug, steamed open and ate after dipping them in melted butter. We strained the broth, which usually had its share of sand, and drank that.

The south side of the island also offered a relatively sheltered cove where small boats could drift on moorings and where the substrate was muddy - the perfect setting for the hard shelled (quahog) clam beds. Here we waded in water up to our knees, and sometimes deeper, and felt into the mud with our feet. The clams felt like rocks and were plentiful. This hard shelled variety we ate raw with lemon juice and ketchup as the sauce.

The surrounding rocky ledges sheltered multitudes of orange-brown rock crabs and the mud flats were also a feeding and spawning ground for the blue-clawed crab.

The nearby swampy shoreline consisted of a thick thousand year old sedge composed of the compacted roots of the ubiquitous eel grass. The edges of this sedge were laced with holes which were home to thousands of Fiddler crabs. These we also gathered for bait in order to catch "blackfish" (tautog) and to fish for flounder and sometimes eel.

Where the crab holes weakened the sedge, chunks of it would break off and gradually disintegrate because of tidal action. Here we found quartz arrowheads which had been lost eons ago by local indian hunters after the migrating geese and ducks which, in earlier times, passed through in uncountable numbers.

This was the perfect place for a kid to grow up, and was a compliment to the other seven months of the year when we lived in the middle Bronx in a fifth floor apartment in a building which had no elevators. Yes, the sea and seafood were ingrained in me from my earliest years and then reinforced by 24 years in the Navy, 5 years in the Scuba and Baja tour business and finally by years of fishing and exploring using inflatable boats, canoes and kayaks. It has been a good and exciting seafaring life.

The Old San Diego Lighthouse

CALAMARI

Overleaf:
Calamari in Situ

CALAMARI (Squid)

RECIPES IN THIS SECTION

THE SQUID YEARS

It was 1971. I was 60 feet underwater in the La Jolla Canyon, off San Diego. The squid were spawning, and it was hard to believe that so many small shimmering bodies could appear in one place at one time. The market squid off the California coast are the species, Loligo opalescens. And here were millions of them, mating, laying eggs, radiating in ever changing colors, darting here and there, and being eaten by every predatory beast in the ocean. Crabs feasted, tearing apart the dying bodies of the squid which had spawned (the species off California dies after spawning). Phalanxes of bull-nosed rays flew through the breeding melee in squadron-like formations gorging as they went. Random blue sharks swam by with squid bodies and pieces dribbling from their overstuffed jaws. It was a giant seafood festival as every other fish in the vicinity joined the feast. This spawning mass was a sight never to be forgotten, and for me it was the mental beginning of this book.

Cousteau had spoken of this spawning behavior in one of his films, referring to the squid as "Sea Arrows". He made it a point to compliment the chef aboard his ship, the Calypso, for his genius in preparing this abundant food in so many different ways, yet I had never eaten squid. Now I was intrigued by the idea. Here was an ocean full of food, but I did not know how to prepare, cook or serve it. The search for the answers provided a lot of culinary excitement. My children refer to this period as "The squid years!"

Although 1971 is not too long ago, squid has since become a far better known and much more utilized resource. I expect that one reason has been the general tendency to change the name to "Calamari" on restaurant menus (and on this chapter). I am certain that diners know that calamari is squid, but perhaps it is more comforting to eat it under a foreign name. Additionally, people have become far more adventuresome in their seafood eating habits in the past twenty years and have finally, and happily, discovered this low calorie, inexpensive and versatile seafood.

Whole squid can be obtained in most markets where sea food is sold. It tends to be less costly in Asian markets where it is sold in much greater quantities. Squid are more perishable than most sea foods, so when a trawler hauls in a net full of squid it is flash-frozen almost immediately after it comes on board. Stores where squid are sold usually receive them as a frozen block, then defrost them for display and sale.

These small squid are generally sold whole and must usually be cleaned by the consumer after purchase (see instructions below). Cleaning is not a difficult chore, but it is a bit time consuming and somewhat messy. For this reason you can sometimes find "cleaned" squid in the market. This increases the cost by about 100%, but it saves time and there is no waste to the final consumer.

CLEANING CALAMARI

A calamari is essentially a two part animal. One part consists of the tube-like mantle with attached fins and internal translucent "pen". The second part consists of the ten arms with head and connecting viscera. The two long arms are tentacles, and eight shorter ones are called sessile arms

To prepare the animal for cooking simply grasp the mantle in one hand and the head in the other and gently pull apart. Lay the head portion in the sink, out of the way, and squeeze the mantle from the tail forward to remove any residual matter (row, etc.) Rinse the inside under running water.

Remove the internal translucent cartilaginous pen from the mantle. To do this, reach up into the top forward end of the mantle with your fingernail and carefully pull it out. If it does not come out in one piece you can sometimes probe inside with your little finger and coax the remaining piece or pieces forward. Alternatively cut a quarter inch off the tail of the mantle and pull the pen parts out that way.

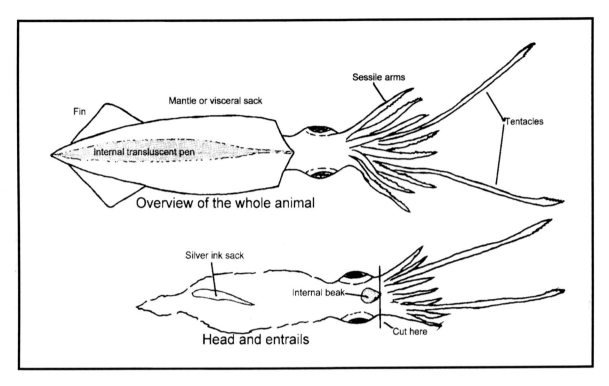

Overview of the whole animal

Head and entrails

Remove the speckled outer skin by grasping the mantle, then with the thumb and forefinger of the other hand pinch the surface until the skin breaks. Peel it off lengthwise. You can now cut the mantle into rings or leave it whole for stuffing. Note: for large squid the skin is not removed so easily. The mantle must be dipped into boiling water for 10 seconds. This loosens the skin and makes easy peeling possible.

Clean the arms by cutting them off just below the eyes. Squeeze the top mass of the arms to force out the small round muscle which contains the beak. Rinse. You do not skin the arms.

If you have a recipe which calls for cooking the squid "in its own ink", the ink sack is located above the eyes, attached to the entrails. In the ocean the squid uses this ink as a decoy when it is attempting to avoid a predator. The ink sack is silvery in color and about an inch long. Cut it away whole for later use.

ALTERNATE CLEANING METHOD

If you do not need the mantles for stuffing, or if you will not need the meat in rings, there is another way to clean calamari which is faster. I discovered this technique while watching the seafood vendors cleaning calamari in bulk at Fisherman's Wharf in San Francisco. The technique is simple. Remove the tentacles as above, then insert a long knife down into the mantle and slit it open. Lay the opened mantle on a flat surface skin side down, and with the side of the knife scrape the meat clean. This will remove all of the remaining viscera and the pen. Flip the meat over and pull off the skin. Rinse and use the meat as desired. Clean the tentacles as described above. If you are making calamari strips this is an excellent way to prepare the meat.

You can save all the discard material and plant it in the garden where it makes fine concentrated fertilizer. Don't plant it where dogs can dig it up. I once had a friend who left his malamute at my house for a weekend. This pup found and dug up, not only the calamari debris, but the trimmings from the many fish I had filleted during the past month. It was a ripe backyard, and washing the dog was an adventure.

Stuffing squid is a chore which can be made a lot easier by making a simple stuffing tool. Buy a plastic baster and discard the rubber top. Cut an inch and a half (3.8 cm) off the pointed end to enlarge the hole. Save the cut off piece. Purchase a cloth cake-decorating funnel and cut a hole in the end just large enough for the body of the baster to fit. Find a $^1/_4$ inch dowel or buy a long cooking chopstick and force it into the cut off end of the baster to make a pushing tool. Now you can add your squid stuffing to the cloth bag, insert the end of the baster into the squid body and squeeze in the stuffing as desired. The pushing rod comes in handy to force any remaining stuffing mix into the baster.

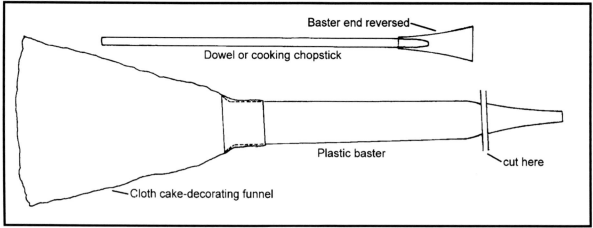

Calamari Stuffing Tool

BASIC CALAMARI COOKING

It is a truism that you must either cook calamari a little or a lot. Less than 1 minute or more than 20 is the guiding rule. Anything in between will result in very tough meat.

The easiest way to ready your calamari for use is to drop the cleaned meat all at once into a pot of boiling water. Let the water return to a boil, then immediately drain in a colander. Run cold water over the meat to stop the cooking. The blanched calamari can now be used cold in salads and similar dishes, or added to hot dishes for its flavor and protein value. It can also be used in recipes which require long cooking times.

CALAMARI AND PLANTAIN CHOWDER

  1 tablespoon olive oil
$^1/_2$ cup chopped yellow onion
  2 finely chopped cloves garlic
$^1/_2$ cup chopped tomato
  1 seeded and chopped jalapeño pepper
$^1/_2$ cup chopped cilantro
$^1/_2$ cup chopped green bell pepper
  1 (8 ounce) can tomato sauce
  1 cup dry red wine
  1 cup water
$^1/_2$ teaspoon thyme
$^1/_2$ teaspoon basil
$^1/_2$ teaspoon oregano
     Juice of one lime
$^1/_2$ teaspoon freshly ground pepper
     Salt to taste
  6 cleaned and blanched calamari and tentacles
  1 cooked and cubed plantain (see directions below)

Heat the oil and sauté the onion and garlic in a large sauce pan for one minute. Add the remaining ingredients and bring to a boil. Lower the heat and simmer for 45 minutes. Serve in bowls with crusty garlic bread and a green salad.

Chowder for 2

COOKING PLANTAIN

Plantain is a banana shaped vegetable sometimes found in your local produce market, but almost always found in Asian and Latino markets. To process, cut off the ends and slice through the skin lengthwise on three sides. Peel off the skin and any residual pieces that continue to adhere. Cut the plantain meat in half at the center, then slice each piece in half lengthwise. Bring one quart of water to a boil, add a tablespoon of salt and cook the plantain meat for 20 to 30 minutes. When cooked the fruit will turn a golden yellow and will float during the cooking. When done a knife blade should penetrate easily. Drain, cool and use in many dishes in place of other starches, like potatoes. The cooked meat has the consistency and flavor of a yam or sweet potato with a slight taste of lemon.

CALAMARI AU GRATIN

    8 cleaned, blanched and sliced calamari
  $^1/_2$ cup sliced yellow onion
  $^1/_2$ cup grated Swiss cheese
  $^1/_2$ cup chopped fresh parsley
    1 tablespoon fresh rosemary
       Salt and pepper to taste
    2 tablespoons melted butter
  $^1/_2$ cup milk
    1 tablespoon Dijon style mustard

In an oven-proof dish layer half the calamari, onion, cheese, parsley and rosemary. Sprinkle on the salt and freshly ground pepper. Repeat the layering with the remainder of the first five ingredients. Pour on the melted butter, then the the milk/mustard mixture. Cover with plastic wrap and microwave on high for 12 minutes. Serve hot with a green vegetable and salad.

Serves 2

CALAMARI BISQUE

This bisque is a wonderful way to combine the flavors of asparagus and mild licorice taste from the anise with calamari. Garnishing with the cooked tentacles, which assume a flower shape, adds to the appearance and the conversation.

    1 cleaned and chopped leek
    2 chopped cloves garlic
    2 tablespoons butter
    6 cleaned, blanched and chopped calamari (reserve 2 tentacle clusters)
  $^1/_2$ pound washed and cooked asparagus
    1 cup half-and-half
  $^1/_2$ cup finely chopped fresh anise (leaves and root) or $^1/_2$ teaspoon anise seeds
       Salt and pepper to taste

Lightly sauté leek and garlic in butter. Combine with other ingredients (less 2 tentacle clusters) in blender. Purée until mixture is smooth. Heat in saucepan until warm. Serve with toast and green salad. Place one calamari tentacle in the center of each bowl as an edible garnish

Serves 2

CALAMARI STRIPS

Calamari strips are one of my favorite appetizers during cocktail lounge "happy hours" in Southern California. The strips are easy to prepare and make good finger food to accompany a martini or a glass of wine or beer.

Five calamari mantles and cleaned tentacles
- **1 cup flour**
- **2 beaten eggs**
- **2 cups seasoned bread crumbs**
- **1 quart canola oil**
- **2 lemon wedges**
- **Seafood cocktail sauce (pg.157)**
- **Horseradish /sourcream sauce (pg. 153)**

Heat oil to 375 degrees

Lay the calamari mantles out on a plastic bag on a cutting board and cover with another plastic bag. Pound the calamari with a meat mallet to tenderize and break down the fibers. Slice the mantels lengthwise into half inch strips. Dust each of the calamari pieces, including tentacles, with flour, then dip in the beaten egg, then the bread crumbs to coat. Be certain that the oil is heated to 375 degrees and drop in the strips, five or six at a time. Cook for one minute to avoid toughening, then remove with a slotted spoon and drain on absorbent paper towels laid over newspaper. Recheck that the heat has returned to 375 degrees and repeat with the remaining strips. If possible they are best served at once while still hot, but can be covered and set aside for reheating in a pan later. I do not recommend the microwave for reheating as it tends to toughen the pieces.

Serve with a lemon wedge and choice of seafood cocktail sauce or horseradish/sour cream sauce Calamari strips for 2

9

CALIFORNIA CALAMARI SANDWICH

It is a rare diner who does not find this California sandwich a filling treat. More importantly to me, it was the first calamari recipe which appealed to my children. That was more than fifteen years ago when calamari was little known. I was amazed to hear them rhapsodizing about this sandwich which they had purchased at one of the local waterfront fast seafood restaurants. I made it a point to get to this place and try the food. Their praise was justified.

- 2 (3 inch square) tenderized calamari steaks
- 1 cup flour
- 2 beaten eggs
- 2 cups seasoned bread crumbs
- 1 quart canola oil
- 4 slices San Francisco sour dough bread
   Tartar sauce
- 2 lemon wedges

Take each tenderized calamari steak, dip in flour, then the beaten egg, roll in seasoned bread crumbs and deep fry in the heated oil for one minute until crispy and golden. Drain on absorbent paper towels. Serve on sour dough bread with tartar sauce. Place a lemon wedge on each plate for optional use.

Makes 2 sandwiches

CALAMARI WITH HOISIN SAUCE, BROCCOLI AND SNOW PEAS

The key to making stir-fried Asiatic dishes is early preparation with all the ingredients lined up in order of use. Things proceed quickly when stir-frying and you must be able to reach over, grab the item to be used and get it in the pan. Aside from that, the cooking is easy.

- 3 tablespoons Canola oil
- 2 slices peeled ginger
- 1 cup snow peas
- 2 cups broccoli crowns
- 2 chopped green onions
- 1 cup sliced mushrooms
- 3 finely chopped cloves garlic
- 1 teaspoon sugar
   Salt to taste
- $^1/_2$ cup water
- 2 cups blanched and cross-sliced calamari with tentacles
- 2 tablespoons hoisin sauce (Asian markets)
- 2 tablespoon cream sherry
- 1 tablespoon cornstarch

Heat the oil over high heat until quite hot. Add the ginger and submerge in the oil for 5 seconds. Add the peas, broccoli, onions, mushrooms and garlic and stir fry for 15 seconds. Lower the heat to medium and continue to stir fry for 1 more minute. Add the sugar, salt and water, bring to a boil and steam the vegetables for 2 more minutes. Mix in the calamari, hoisin sauce and sherry. Cook until the calamari are heated through. Don't overcook. Mix in the corn starch and continue cooking and stirring until the mixture thickens slightly. Serve with Chinese noodles or rice and a green salad.

2 servings

CALAMARI FLORENTINE

This is an elegant and different way to serve calamari. Though there are a number of ingredients the recipe is simple to prepare and can be made ahead and then heated in the oven before serving.

$^1/_2$ cup cooked spinach
3 chopped green onions
1 tablespoon lemon juice
3 tablespoons butter
2 large chopped cloves garlic
2 tablespoons flour
$^1/_2$ cup half-and-half
2 teaspoons Worcestershire sauce
5 drops Jalapeño Tabasco
2 tablespoons chopped parsley
1 tablespoon dry sherry
Salt and freshly ground pepper
1 cup cleaned and blanched calamari, cut into $^1/_2$ inch rings
Freshly grated Parmesan cheese
Dash of grated nutmeg
2 sprigs of fresh parsley

Heat oven to 350 degrees.

Drain, squeeze and chop spinach. Combine with the chopped green onion, and lemon juice.

Melt the butter and lightly sauté the garlic. Blend in the flour and half-and-half to make a white sauce. Stir in the Worcestershire Sauce, Tabasco, parsley and sherry. Salt and pepper to taste. Cook until slightly thickened and remove from heat.

In a small baking dishes layer in the calamari, spinach and cream sauce. Grate on the Parmesan cheese and sprinkle with nutmeg. Bake in a 350 degree oven for 20 minutes. Remove from oven, top with a sprig of parsley and serve with rice, green vegetable, green salad and chilled white wine.

Serves 2

CALAMARI / AVOCADO / PASTA SALAD

  8 ounces ($^1/_2$ package) small shell pasta
$^1/_4$ cup olive oil
  2 tablespoons tarragon vinegar
  1 ripe avocado
     Juice of $^1/_4$ lime
  6 cleaned, blanched and cross-sliced calamari mantles plus tentacles
  1 chopped Roma tomato
10 sliced black olives
  1 teaspoon garlic powder
     Salt and pepper to taste

Cook the pasta as directed on the package, drain, place in a bowl and pour on the olive oil and vinegar. Remove the meat from the avocado and chop into $^1/_4$ inch pieces. Sprinkle with the lime juice and mix well to keep the avocado from darkening. Add the avocado to the pasta bowl along with all the other ingredients. Mix well, cover with plastic wrap and place in the refrigerator for three hours or more to blend the flavors. Serve chilled.

Pasta salad for 4

CALAMARI IN SOY SAUCE

$^1/_4$ cup soy sauce
$^1/_4$ cup sugar
6   cleaned and blanched calamari cut into $^1/_2$ inch rings
1   brick of tofu cut into $^1/_2$ inch squares.
2   sliced green onions

Mix soy sauce and sugar and bring to a boil. Reduce heat. Add calamari, tofu and green onion and simmer 20 minutes. Serve with rice and a vegetable. May be prepared ahead of time and served cold.

Serves 2

JAPANESE STYLE SEASONED CALAMARI

6 cleaned and blanched calamari mantles plus tentacles
2 tablespoons soy sauce
2 tablespoons Japanese mirin wine (or cream sherry)
2 tablespoons chopped sweet pickled ginger (Asian markets) or 3 teaspoons fresh grated ginger
1 teaspoon sugar

Cut the calamari into $^1/_2$ inch rings. Leave tentacles whole or if large cut into halves. Combine the remaining ingredients and pour over the calamari. Mix to coat all the meat evenly. Let the coated mixture marinate in the refrigerator for one hour before serving on crackers as an appetizer.

Appetizers for 4

CALAMARI AND TOFU WITH SWEET CHILI SAUCE

Here is a fast low-calorie lunch with enough bite in it to be interesting. The sweet chili sauce is an Asian concoction of red chilies, salt, sugar and vinegar and has a sweet hot pepper flavor.

- 4 (3 ounce) slices of firm tofu
- 2 sliced green onions
- 4 cleaned and blanched calamari mantles plus tentacles
- 4 tablespoons sweet chili sauce. (Asian markets)
- 2 tablespoons fresh grated coconut

Arrange each slice of tofu on a plate and cut into $^3/_4$ inch cubes. Combine with the sliced green onion. Slice the calamari mantles into $^1/_2$ inch rings and chop the tentacles roughly. Mix the calamari with the tofu and cover with two tablespoons chili sauce and a tablespoon of grated coconut. Mix well and serve.

Serves 2

CALAMARI STUFFED WITH SHRIMP AND MUSHROOMS

- 6 cleaned calamari mantles
- 1 cup tomato based spaghetti sauce
- $^1/_2$ cup freshly grated Parmesan cheese for topping

STUFFING

- Finely chopped calamari tentacles
- $^1/_4$ cup finely chopped shrimp
- $^1/_4$ cup finely chopped mushrooms
- $^1/_4$ cup unseasoned bread crumbs or crushed saltines
- 2 tablespoons grated Romano or Parmesan cheese
- 3 finely diced cloves garlic
- 2 tablespoons minced parsley
- $^1/_4$ teaspoon crushed dried oregano
- $^1/_4$ teaspoon coarse ground pepper
- 1 tablespoon cream sherry
- 1 beaten egg
- Pinch salt

Leave calamari mantles whole. Chop calamari tentacles and mix with remaining stuffing ingredients. Using the stuffing tool described on page 6, or a small spoon, stuff calamari mantles with the mixture until $^3/_4$ full and pin the ends of the mantles together with toothpicks. (Calamari mantles shrink between 30 and 40 percent with cooking so do not overfill). Pour half the spaghetti sauce in a baking dish and lay out the calamari in a single layer. Cover with the remaining sauce and sprinkle with Parmesan cheese. Bake covered at 350 degrees for 30 minutes then uncover for 5 more to melt the cheese. Serve with rice and mixed vegetables.

Serves 2

STUFFED CALAMARI ROCKEFELLER

>   10   cleaned calamari mantles
>   **STUFFING**
>   1   cup cooked couscous
>   1   cup cooked spinach, squeeze dry and chopped
>   1   chopped green onion
> 1 $^{1}/_{2}$ tablespoons Pernod or Anisette liquor
> $^{1}/_{2}$ teaspoon paprika
> $^{1}/_{2}$ teaspoon garlic powder
>   Salt and coarse ground pepper
>   2   tablespoons melted butter (divided use)

Heat oven to 350 degrees.

To make the stuffing combine the first seven ingredients and one tablespoon of the melted butter and mix well. Fill each of the calamari mantles $^{2}/_{3}$ full with the stuffing mixture and pin the opening with a toothpick. Place the stuffed mantles in an oven-proof baking dish in one layer. Dribble the second tablespoon of the melted butter over the top. Bake uncovered in a 350 degree oven for 20 minutes. Baste half way through with the pan drippings. The most attractive way to serve stuffed calamari is to slice it into disks which are tastefully arranged on the plate with a suitable garnish of complimentary color such as pimiento strips or thin sliced tomato. Serve hot with a green vegetable and rice or sea shell pasta.

Serves 2

TEXAS STYLE STUFFED CALAMARI

>   6   cleaned calamari mantles
>   **STUFFING**
>   6   peeled medium shrimp
>   2   seeded jalapeño peppers, sliced lengthwise into quarters
> $^{1}/_{4}$ cup Mozzarella cheese cut in strips
>   1   recipe for caper sauce (Pg. 151)

Heat oven to 350 degrees

Stuff each calamari body with a shrimp, a strip of green chili, and a thin strip of cheese. Pin the ends with toothpicks. Place stuffed calamari side by side in an oven-proof dish, top with caper sauce and bake covered in the oven for 20 minutes. Serve with green salad, rice and asparagus.

Serves 2

TERIYAKI CALAMARI STEAKS ON THE GRILL

Interestingly, the first time I had anything like this was at the great castle in Osaka, Japan. I was just inside, walking along the main moat when a family appeared eating flapping pieces of calamari the way our teen-agers eat beef jerky. I wandered down to the area from whence they had come and found an old man tending the Japanese version of a back yard barbecue layered with cooking calamari. I don't remember how much each piece cost - not much - but I do remember walking along with the crowd chewing on this soy sauce darkened meat and not even having one curious person look at me. I have since duplicated this dish, but using the much larger South American calamari which can sometimes be found in Asian markets.

Large calamari are much tougher than the small table calamari from California and take more preparation when cleaning. Pull out the arms and slit the body down the bottom center. Remove the pen and scrape and wash the inside of the body. Remove the outer skin by dropping the meat in boiling water for 10 seconds then peel the skin from the flesh. Boil the tentacles for 25 minutes, drain and cool. Reserve these for calamari strips. Cut the body into square steaks.

Prepare and light the barbecue

- **2 calamari steaks from large calamari**
- **2 cups teriyaki sauce**
- **2 pressed cloves garlic**
- **1 tablespoon fresh grated ginger**

Cover the skinned calamari steaks with a plastic bag and pound hard with a meat tenderizing mallet until limp and pliable. Add some criss-cross scoring on both sides to retain the marinade. Place the beaten steaks in a bowl and cover each with teriyaki, garlic and ginger. Let the calamari marinate for 30 minutes, turning once or twice to insure even coating. Lift the calamari from the bowl, drain slightly and then place on the barbecue grill about 2 inches from the coals. Turn every minute until both sides are cooked. Marinate periodically to keep moist. Total cooking time should be about 4 to 5 minutes. The barbecued meat can be sliced and eaten as finger food or presented more formally with white rice and pineapple chunks. You can also chill the meat and eat it later as I did in Japan.

Makes calamari steaks for 2

THAI CALAMARI AND SHRIMP

- 2 tablespoons sesame oil
- 1 chopped green onion
- 2 chopped mushrooms
- 3 chopped cloves garlic
- $^1/_2$ cup chopped celery
- 1 or 2 seeded and chopped jalapeño peppers
- 1 shredded small carrot
- 1 tablespoon chopped pickled ginger (Asiatic markets) or 2 teaspoons fresh grated ginger Juice $^1/_2$ lime
- $^1/_2$ cup chopped cilantro
- 1 teaspoon sugar
- 1 tablespoon fish sauce (Asian markets)
- 1 tablespoon sweet chili sauce (Asian Markets)
- 2 tablespoon green Thai curry (Asian markets)
- $^1/_2$ cup coconut milk
- 6 peeled and rough chopped medium shrimp
- 4 cleaned, blanched and cross-sliced calamari with tentacles

This is a stir-fried dish, so have everything ready to cook and lined up in proper order.

Heat the oil quite hot. Quickly add the onion, mushrooms, garlic, celery, jalapeño peppers and carrot. Stir fry for one minute. Add the pickled ginger, lime juice, cilantro, sugar and fish sauce. Bring to a simmer and add the chili sauce, the green Thai curry, coconut milk, chopped shrimp and calamari. Return to a simmer and stir until the shrimp are uniformly pink and the calamari heated through. Serve over rice and place two calamari tentacle blossoms on each plate. A green salad and chilled white wine make a perfect meal.

Serves 2

CALAMARI WITH BROCCOLI AND SOUR CREAM

- 1 finely diced clove garlic
- 1 cup of rough chopped cooked broccoli
- $^1/_2$ cup chopped parsley
- 1 tablespoon butter
- 6 cleaned, blanched and cross-sliced calamari mantles
- $^1/_2$ pint sour cream
  Grated Parmesan cheese
- 2 lime wedges (optional)

Mix the first three ingredients and sauté in melted butter for 2 minutes. Mix in the calamari and sour cream and heat until warmed through. Sprinkle with Parmesan to taste. Squeeze on lime juice if desired. Serve with rice and thin slices of tomato as a garnish.

Serves 2

CALAMARI FRITTERS

    8 cleaned, blanched and finely chopped calamari plus tentacles
$^1/_2$ cup vegetable oil
     SAUCE

    1 teaspoon cornstarch
    2 tablespoons cold water
    1 cup applesauce
$^1/_2$ teaspoon grated lemon peel
    3 teaspoons sugar
    2 tablespoons ketchup
    4 drops Tabasco sauce
    1 teaspoon curry powder
    1 tablespoon finely diced sweet pickled ginger (Asian markets)
     BATTER
$^1/_4$ cup flour
    1 beaten egg
$^1/_4$ cup water
$^1/_4$ cup tomato sauce
$^1/_2$ cup bread crumbs

Heat oil to 375 degrees

Prepare the sauce: combine the cornstarch with the cold water. Mix with applesauce and cook for 2 minutes. Add the lemon peel, sugar, ketchup and Tabasco sauce and stir well.

Prepare the batter by combining the listed ingredients. Blend until smooth. Add the chopped calamari and form into patties. Fry in 375 degree oil in a single layer for 30 seconds on each side or until golden brown. Drain on absorbent paper. Serve hot with the prepared sauce as an appetizer.

Appetizers for 4

CALAMARI COLE SLAW

    6 cleaned, blanched and chopped calamari
    2 cups finely shredded red or green cabbage
    2 tablespoons grated red onion
    1 grated carrot
$^1/_2$ cup lite mayonnaise
    2 tablespoons dry dill weed
    1 tablespoon lemon or lime juice
$1^1/_2$ teaspoons sugar or substitute $^1/_2$ packet NutraSweet (Equal)
     Salt and pepper to taste

Mix all ingredients thoroughly and let stand in refrigerator several hours or overnight to blend flavors.

Makes salad for 4

CALAMARI WITH BAMBOO SHOOTS

2	tablespoons butter
4	finely chopped cloves garlic
1	tablespoon freshly grated ginger
1/2	cup sliced bamboo shoots
1	chopped green onion
1	tablespoon soy sauce
1	tablespoon cream sherry
4	cleaned, blanched and chopped calamari
	Salt and pepper to taste

Melt the butter in a sauce pan and sauté the garlic and ginger for 30 seconds over medium heat. Add the bamboo shoots and green onions and sauté for an additional 30 seconds. Mix in the soy sauce and sherry and add the calamari. Cook for about 1 minute to warm the calamari. Remove from the heat and serve over rice with fresh green peas and a green salad.

Serves 2

GINGERED CALAMARI

2	tablespoons canola oil
1/2	cup chopped onion
1	cup chopped bok choy cabbage
1	seeded and finely chopped jalapeño pepper
1/2	cup fresh or thawed frozen peas
2	tablespoons grated fresh ginger
1/4	cup water
1/4	cup soy sauce
1	tablespoon sugar
6	cleaned, blanched and chopped calamari

This is a stir-fry recipe so have all the materials ready. Heat the oil in a wok or large frying pan until quite hot. Add the onions, cabbage and jalapeño and stir-fry for 30 seconds. Add the peas and ginger and stir-fry for an additional 30 seconds. Pour in the water and soy sauce and spoon in the sugar. Mix well and reduce the heat to medium. Add the calamari and stir together just long enough to heat the calamari through. Serve with rice.

Serves 2

CLAMS

Overleaf:

A Cluster of Quahogs

CLAMS

RECIPES IN THIS SECTION

One of the highlights of my year in Vietnam was the discovery of a large nest of clams on an island 180 miles south of Saigon in the South China Sea. Although I was assigned to General Westmoreland's staff, I was still a Naval aviator on flight orders and was therefore required to fly a certain number of hours every month. This was a wonderful arrangement for me. Staff duty was never my finest hour, and the flight requirement would get me away from the desk and the Saigon smog several days of every month. I was flying a small two engine transport and would only discover my flight destination when I checked in for the day. Shortly after my first month in the area the operations folks asked me to fly the mail to a small U.S. Coast Guard detachment on the Island of Conson to the south. This was an easy over-water flight and the approach was uncomplicated since there was almost no air traffic in the area. The short runway was at the northern end of the island and ran east-west from one side of the island to the other. The place was picturesque and the breezes were balmy, and since this was the first Vietnamese location I had visited that was not a danger zone or polluted, I decided to strip to my underwear and take a swim. Both ends of the runway had beaches so I strolled to the nearest one and walked in. The water was about 80 degrees Fahrenheit and the swimming was great. It was obvious that the water was unpolluted, so it occurred to me that there might be clams hidden away in the sand. I began shuffling my feet into the sub-strate the way we did in the mud flats around Long Island. Sure enough, I began to feel small rock-like items which turned out to be an abundance of inch and half wide "butter clams". Bonanza! I gathered up perhaps fifty and carried them back to Saigon where my roommate and I shucked and ate them. It helped that he was a native of Maine. All we had was lemon juice, ketchup and martinis, but that was all we needed. The feast was welcome. I made that flight five more times before returning to the U.S. It was the most favored destination and I am reminded of it each time I have small clams on the half shell.

ABOUT CLAMS

SOFT SHELL STEAMER CLAMS

Thin shelled steamer clams are found in many coastal areas of the United States. In my native New York we used to find them on the mud flats and sand bars at low tide. A thrown rock would produce a tell-tale upright squirt of water from the clams as they hastily withdrew their siphons. This would tell us where to dig and we would fill a pail with clams in short order.

Long Island Sound used to have vast beds of these clams, but pollution has taken its toll and the clams from the Bronx end of the Sound can be dangerous. Most now come from other locations.

If you can obtain them, steam them open and dip them into melted butter. This way they are the epitome of clam perfection.

THE EASTERN HARD SHELL CLAM

The clam you are most likely to encounter in markets throughout the United States is the Eastern hard clam. It may be called quahog (an indian name pronounced KO hog), chowder clam, cherrystone or littleneck, depending on size and the locality where you obtain them. Quahog is a generic name that loosely applies to this clam in all sizes. "Chowder clam" refers to the largest of the species measuring from 3 to 5 inches across the shell, "Cherrystone" falls into the size range from 2 to 3 inches, and "Littlenecks" measure in below 2 inches and smaller.

One of the interesting aspects of the Quahog clam is its formal Latin name (Venus mercinaria). This was derived from the intense blue colored part of the inner shell which was used by the native Americans to make beads or wampum for trading. The white part of the shell was also used for wampum beads but these had about half the value of the darker blue ones.

As a kid on Long Island Sound we used to go out barefooted and feel around in the mud for these mollusks. It was exciting because both "blue-claw" and "spider" crabs would also submerge themselves in the mud (not often, but enough to make us worry) and that "rock" you felt *might* be a crab instead of a clam. As with the steamer clams mentioned above, there were lots of hard shelled clams back then, and they were uncontaminated. Now there are far fewer clams and contamination in the Sound near New York City is a problem. Fortunately, there are still plenty of areas in New England and elsewhere where unpolluted "venus" clams can be obtained.

With hard shelled clams size makes a difference both in cost and texture. The smaller clams command a higher price because they are both bite-sized and tender. The larger "chowder" clams are tougher and become more palatable when chopped into smaller pieces and used in cooking.

In that sense, on the West Coast the famous "Pismo" is by nature a very large clam, yet down in Mexico, in Baja, it is often eaten raw in clam cocktails. Street vendors prepare and sell cups full, mixed with lemon or lime, salsa and cilantro. The Baja Pismo clam cocktail recipe is found below.

The Pismo (Tivela stultorum) derives its colloquial name from the area of Pismo Beach, California where they were once numerous. A more suitable name might be Pacific Coast Surf Clam. This clam is still abundant down in Baja, and it is probable that the people in the region also have a special name for this great clam. The shells can measure over 7 inches in length and are sometimes half an inch thick so they are heavy and the meat is plentiful. Most sold in the market measure about 5 inches. As an aside, you may discover a small dowel shaped object in the flesh that looks like clear plastic. This peculiar object is natural and permits the clam to digest starch.

OPENING CLAMS

There is no great secret to opening clams. Essentially you force a knife blade between the shells, cut the two adductor muscles and then pull or pry the two halves apart. To do this, wash the clams to remove any dirt, then let them sit ten or so minutes. Like any muscle, the adductor can only maintain full strength for a limited period of time, then it relaxes. Gently pick up the rested clam and place on your hand so that the hinge is toward the palm. (see illustration) Place the knife blade in the crack between the two

halves then apply pressure on the blade with your four fingers. If the blade does not quickly slide between the shell halves rock the blade a bit as you continue to squeeze with your fingers. Eventuality the knife should push the two halves apart so that you can slide in the end of the blade. Once inside cut first one adductor muscle and then the other. These muscles are on the right and left side of the clam. The two shell halves can then be pulled apart. Discard the empty one. The clam meat will still be anchored to the other half of the shell. Finish the job by sliding the blade under the meat and cutting the clam free.

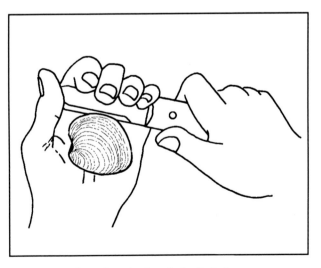

Opening the hard-shelled clam

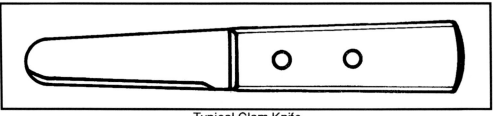

Typical Clam Knife

CLAMS ON THE HALF SHELL

The opened clam can now be served on the half shell. The usual technique is to place the clams in their shells on crushed ice. Serve them with a lemon wedge, a cocktail fork and seafood cocktail sauce (pg. 157).

BAJA SURF CLAM COCKTAIL

In Baja you will find street vendors with small white carts serving these delicious clam cocktails in plastic cups. The clams they use come from the western side of the Baja peninsular well away from any contamination. We have often watched Mexican fishermen diving for them along the Pacific coast north of Cedros Island. As they collect the clams they fill gunny sacks with the catch. On return to their villages the fishermen deposit the sacks off the beach in the ocean with their personal markers on them. Here they await the collecting truck from Ensenada. When the truck is due, they retrieve their catch and sell it. The truck trip from the mid-Baja area to Ensenada takes about eight hours so the clams are ocean fresh when they arrive. They are delivered to the Government run open-air fish market. Each morning the individual street-corner vendors buy their supplies and set out to their chosen location. The cocktails are expensive by Mexican standards, but they are super fresh, sell rapidly and continuously. To me they are the highlight of a quick Baja visit. The large Eastern Quahog clams can be substituted if Pismos are not available.

- 2   large Pacific surf clams (or four chowder quahogs)
- 1   teaspoon lime juice
- 2   tablespoons of red Mexican salsa
- 1   tablespoon of chopped cilantro
- 1   tablespoon finely chopped red onion
- 1   dash of Tabasco sauce (optional)

Shuck the clams over a bowl to catch the juice and rinse the meat thoroughly to remove any residual sand. Cut out the stomach and discard. Chop the remaining clam meat into half-inch pieces and add to the clam liquid. Be certain to cut the clam buttons from the shell (the adductor mussels) and add them to the meat. Squeeze in the lime juice, add salsa, cilantro, green onion and Tabasco sauce - if using. Mix and serve cold in a plastic cup with a plastic spoon for authenticity.

Makes 1 hearty clam cocktail

CLAM SANDWICH

       3 cups canola oil
          The meat from 12 steamer clams
       1 beaten raw egg
       1 cup of seasoned or unseasoned dried bread crumbs
       4 slices San Francisco sour dough bread
          Tartar sauce (Pg.158)

Heat the oil in a deep fat fryer to 375 degrees. Put the bread crumbs in a gallon sized plastic food storage bag. Dip each piece of clam meat in the beaten egg, drain then place in the plastic bag with the crumbs. When all the clam pieces have been added, coat the clams with the crumbs by shaking the bag. Remove the clams to a separate dish, then place half of them in the heated fat. Cook for about 3 minutes until golden then remove with a slotted spoon. Let the oil return to 375 degrees and deep fry the remaining clams. Let the clams drain for a few minutes on a paper towel placed on some folded newspaper. Spread a layer of tartar sauce on two slices of sour dough bread, then place six of the drained clams on each piece and cover with the other bread slices. Cut each sandwich in half and serve.

You can also serve these fried clams as hors d'oeuvres by placing dollops of tartar sauce on $1\,{}^{1}/_{2}$ inch toasted squares of bread and anchoring the clams in place with a toothpick. Make in advance and keep warm in a 200 degree oven. Makes 2 sandwiches

CLAMS CASINO

      12 medium hard shelled clams
       3 tablespoons butter
       1 large finely chopped mushroom
       1 finely chopped medium onion
       2 finely chopped cloves garlic
    $^{1}/_{4}$ cup bread crumbs (seasoned if desired)
       1 tablespoon lemon juice
    $^{1}/_{4}$ cup chopped parsley leaves
          Freshly ground black pepper to taste
       2 strips of uncooked bacon cut into 1 inch pieces
          Lemon wedges

Heat oven to 375 degrees and prepare a rectangular oven proof dish with a half inch layer of rock salt.

Open the clams and discard one of the two shells. Cut the adductor muscles on the other shell so that the meat is free. For large clams cut the meat into halves or quarters. Smaller cherrystone clams are best. Place the clams in their shells and press the shells into the rock salt to balance them. Sauté the mushrooms, onion and garlic in melted butter. Remove from heat and mix in the bread crumbs, lemon juice, parsley and pepper. Spoon the mixture around and over the clams, then top each with a piece of bacon.

Bake in the pre-heated oven for 10 minutes. Remove pan and place about 3 inches under a broiler for about a minute or two until the bacon is crisp. Serve on rock salt with lemon wedges. Serves 2

CLAMS AU GRATIN

This dish is a marvelous treat which I first had in the El Rey Sol restaurant in Ensenada, Mexico where the large pismo clams come in fresh almost daily. The El Rey Sol specializes in French cuisine, so presumably this dish has French roots.

- 3 Pismo or 4 large chowder clams
- 3 tablespoons butter
- 1 tablespoon flour
- $1/4$ cup half-and-half
- 2 finely chopped cloves garlic
- 1 finely chopped green onion
- 1 tablespoon chopped pimiento
- 1 tablespoon dry vermouth
- $1/3$ cup grated parmesan cheese
  Salt and pepper to taste
  Rock salt for baking dish

Open the clams and remove the meat. Discard the stomach portion. Rinse the meat to rid it of sand then coarsely chop. Set aside. Wash the shells.

Melt the butter in a sauce pan and blend in the flour. Add the half-and-half, clam meat, garlic, onion, pimiento and vermouth and cook over low heat until the mixture thickens slightly. Remove from the heat and stir in all but one tablespoon of the parmesan cheese. The reserved portion will be used for topping. Spoon the mixture into four of the shell halves and top with the reserved parmesan. Place the shells in an oven-proof dish on rock salt and broil for about 5 minutes until the surface cheese is lightly browned. Serve with saffron rice and a green salad.

Serves 2

CHOWDERS

If you know anything at all about chowders you know that everyone has their own favorite recipe. There are whole books on chowders and whole lists of ingredients that can be added at the whim of the chef. The chowders below are made the way I like them, they are reasonably simple, tasty and filling. What more can you ask?

CLAM CHOWDER - MANHATTAN

This is the red chowder I was brought up on. We would gather our own clams, shuck them and chop them up for the chowder. This chowder always made a welcome filling dish on cool Fall days.

   5 slices of bacon, cooked crisp and crumbled
   1 chopped large onion
   3 chopped or pressed cloves garlic
   2 tablespoons olive oil
   2 cups boiling water
   4 red potatoes, cut into $^3/_4$ inch cubes
  12 hard shelled clams, chopped, plus juice (or)
   4 (6.5 ounce) cans chopped clams plus juice
   1 (14.5 ounce) can of whole peeled tomatoes, crushed
   1 (8 ounce) can tomato sauce
$^1/_2$ cup red wine
   2 teaspoons dried thyme
   2 bay leaves
$^1/_2$ teaspoon sugar
$^1/_2$ teaspoon coarse ground pepper
     Salt to taste

In a Dutch oven cook the bacon until crisp, drain and discard fat and set bacon strips aside. Crumble when cool. Sauté the onion and garlic in the olive oil until the onion is translucent, add water and potatoes and simmer for fifteen minutes to cook the potatoes. Add the crumbled bacon and remaining ingredients and simmer for an additional fifteen minutes. If I have clams in the shell I often add them with the bacon and let them open in the chowder. I then remove the shells and chop the meat. Steaming them in the chowder saves all the juices. If possible let the chowder sit for a day in the refrigerator since the flavor improves with age. Remove bay leaves before serving. Serve with French or sour dough bread. Note: you can substitute mussels for clams which results in a slight change in flavor.

Serves 4

CLAM CHOWDER - NEW ENGLAND

This chowder is so different from the red Manhatten chowder (previous page), that it falls into an entirely different taste category. As the name indicates, this is a New England chowder. I was first introduced to it in Rhode Island when the Navy sent me there in 1944. Initially I was suspicious. It didn't look like my kind of chowder but the smell was wonderful. The learning process was rapid and I now find that I often order this white chowder instead of the chowder of my youth.

     5   slices of bacon, cooked crisp and crumbled
     2   tablespoons butter or margarine
     2   tablespoons olive oil
   $1/2$ cup chopped onion
     2   finely chopped cloves garlic
     4   large potatoes, lightly boiled and diced
     1   cup bottled clam juice
     1   cup water
    12   hard shelled clams, chopped, plus juice, or
     4   (6.5 ounce) cans chopped clams with juice
     1   quart milk
     1   tablespoon thyme
   $1/4$ teaspoon white pepper
     3   dashes Tabasco sauce (optional)
         Salt to taste

In a Dutch oven cook bacon until crisp, drain fat, remove from the pan and set aside. Crumble when cool. Melt butter and combine with olive oil, then sauté the onion and garlic until the onion is translucent. Add the potatoes, clam juice and water and bring to a boil. Add the clams, bacon, milk and remaining ingredients. Heat to a simmer but do not boil. Serve with salad and crusty French or Italian bread. Note: you can substitute mussels for clams in this recipe.

Serves 4

CLAM CHOWDER - PACIFIC COAST SURF CLAM

This chowder utilizes the large surf clams of the Pacific coast and incorporates some of the typical spices and herbs that are characteristic of the food of the Southwest. Once again, it is a different but equally delicious chowder.

     4   medium red potatoes, cut into $3/4$ inch cubes
     3   cups water
     3   large Pacific surf clams (or 6 large quahogs)
   $1/2$ cup chopped onion
     3   tablespoons dry vermouth
   $1/2$ cup chopped cilantro
     1   cup chopped fresh mushrooms
     1   cup half-and-half

  2 **tablespoons butter**
  1 **teaspoon crushed red pepper bits**
     Dash of paprika

Boil the potatoes in three cups of water for about 15 minutes until cooked but still firm. Drain but reserve the cooking liquid. Steam the clams in the reserved potato water with the chopped onion and 3 tablespoons of dry sherry until the clams open. Set aside to cool, then remove the meat. Rinse the meat to remove sand and chop into half inch chunks. Discard the shells.

In a medium sauce pan combine the potatoes, potato water, clams and clam juices with the remaining ingredients and bring to a simmer. Ladle into deep soup bowls, sprinkle with paprika and float oyster crackers on top. Crusty bread and a green salad compliments.

Serves 4

CLAM-CURRY MANICOTTI WITH TOFU AND SPINACH

  8 **manicotti**
  2 **tablespoons olive oil**
  4 **chopped cloves garlic**
  4 **chopped large mushrooms**
  1 **package frozen spinach, thawed, squeeze dry and chopped**
 $^1/_2$ **cup chopped red pimientos (Pg. 156)**
 $^1/_2$ **pound firm tofu, sliced into $^1/_2$ inch cubes**
  2 **(6.5 ounce) cans chopped clams (or)**
 $^1/_2$ **cup chopped steamer clams (minus juice)**
  1 **teaspoon dried thyme**
     Salt and pepper to taste
     One recipe for curry/sour cream sauce (Pg. 152)

Heat oven to 375 degrees

Cook the manicotti for 6 minutes in lightly salted boiling water. Drain and place in cold water. Set aside. Lightly sauté the garlic in olive oil until cooked but not brown. Mix the garlic with the remaining ingredients (less the curry/lime sauce) in a large bowl and spoon the mixture into the manicotti shells. Place the stuffed manicotti in a greased oven proof dish and layer on the curry/lime sauce. Bake covered in a 375 degree oven for 30 minutes. Serve with a green salad.

Serves 2

CLAM SAUCE WITH PASTA

Clams combine nicely with other ingredients to make wonderful sauces for spaghetti or other pasta.

- **1 tablespoon butter**
- **1 tablespoon olive oil**
- **2 large finely chopped cloves garlic**
- **$^1/_2$ medium tomato, chopped**
- **$^1/_2$ bottle clam juice**
- **2 (6.5 ounce) cans chopped clams, drained**
- **3 sliced mushrooms**
- **$^1/_4$ cup dry white wine**
- **1 dash Tabasco sauce or pinch of cayenne pepper**
- **Salt and pepper to taste**
- **$^1/_2$ cup chopped Italian parsley (regular parsley can substitute)**
- **Freshly grated Romano cheese**

Melt oils to blend, add garlic and lightly sauté. Add tomato and clam juice and cook until the tomato is soft. Mix in the clams and their juice, mushrooms, wine and spices. Cook down until the liquid is reduced by half. Use additional clam juice to adjust the flavor or consistency if necessary. Serve over pasta with parsley and grated Romano cheese, crusty Italian garlic bread, green salad and a dry red wine. Serves 2

CLAM SAUCE #2 FOR PASTA

- **$^1/_4$ cup olive oil**
- **2 finely chopped cloves garlic**
- **2 (6.5 ounce) cans clams, (reserve juice)**
- **$^1/_4$ teaspoon dry basil leaves and/or oregano**
- **2 tablespoons chopped cilantro**
- **Freshly grated Parmesan cheese**

Sauté garlic in oil until tender. Add clams, clam juice, basil and cilantro. Bring to simmer. Serve over pasta with freshly grated Parmesan cheese, crusty bread and a dry white wine.

Serves 2

CLAM / EGGPLANT SAUCE FOR RICE OR PASTA

- 2 tablespoons olive oil
- $^1/_2$ cup finely diced onion
- 3 pressed cloves garlic
- 1 cup peeled and cubed eggplant
- 1 (8 ounce) can tomato sauce
- $^1/_4$ cup red wine
- $^1/_2$ bottle (4 ounces) clam juice
- 1 rough chopped tomato
- 1 (6.5 ounce) can chopped clams
- 1 teaspoon dried thyme
- 1 teaspoon sugar

Sauté onion and garlic in olive oil until the onion becomes opaque. Add the eggplant, tomato sauce, wine and clam juice. Bring to a boil, lower heat and simmer until the eggplant softens. Stir frequently. Mix in the remaining ingredients and simmer for an additional five minutes . Remove from heat and serve over pasta or rice with a green salad and red wine.

Serves 2

COQUINA BROTH

When I was stationed at the Naval Air Station, Jacksonville, Florida we used to spend weekends down at the Atlantic beaches between Mayport and St. Augustine. It was there that I discovered the small colorful coquina clams which are found throughout the region. They would appear by the thousands when a wave crashed on the beach, then disappear almost as quickly by working their way back into the loose sand with their powerful "foot". You could gather a bucketful in no time by scooping them up with a strainer before they could reroot themselves. They became a culinary treat when we would take them home and use them to make a delicate clam broth.

- 1 pint of fresh water
- 1 ounce dry vermouth
- $^1/_2$ gallon fresh coquina clams
- 2 tablespoons butter

In a deep pan mix the water and vermouth and add the rinsed clams. Cover the pan and turn up the heat to bring the mixture to a boil. Reduce the heat to a simmer to allow all the shells to open. Stir once. Strain the liquid through a sieve to remove the shells and other matter. Mix in the butter and allow it to melt. Serve as a clear broth before a meal with crusty bread for dipping, or use in place of bottled clam juice in cooking.

Serves 2

JAPANESE SPICED CLAMS

Manila clams are small clams about an inch to an inch and a half in length. Despite the name, the bulk of these clams come from the U.S. Pacific Northwest. They are found in many Asian markets, and among other uses, are pickled by the Japanese as a condiment.

20 to 30 fresh Manila clams
 1 cup fresh water
 1 tablespoon soy sauce
 2 tablespoons Japanese mirin wine (or cream sherry)
 1 tablespoon sugar
 1 tablespoon chopped pickled ginger

Steam the clams in a cup of water until open. Remove the clams from the pan and add the other ingredients to the cooking liquid. Turn the heat to low and allow the combined ingredients to come to a simmer. Remove the meat from the steamed clams and chop lightly. Combine with the remaining ingredients and let the mixture cook down until the liquid is reduced by half and all the flavors are blended. Cool and serve with rice and pickled Japanese seaweed as a condiment.

Serves 4

SOFT SHELLED STEAMER CLAMS

 $^1/_2$ gallon live Eastern steamer clams
 2 cups water
 $^1/_4$ pound (1 stick) melted butter

Place the clams and water in a large covered kettle and bring to a boil. Steam the clams for about 5 minutes until the shells are open. Serve with melted butter. Pull each clam from its shell by the neck discarding the neck skin. Dip into the melted butter before eating. Sop up the broth with crusty garlic bread. What more needs to be said about this delicious steamed clam.

Serves 2

STEAMED LITTLENECK OR BUTTER CLAMS

 2 tablespoons butter
 2 chopped green onions
 2 finely chopped cloves garlic
 $^1/_4$ cup chopped cilantro
 2 tablespoons cream sherry
 1 cup of water
 1 teaspoon salt
 1 pound small hard clams in the shell
 2 tablespoons half-and-half
    Crusty French of Italian bread for dipping

Melt the butter in a sauce pan and sauté the onions and garlic for one minute. Add the cilantro, sherry, water and salt and bring to a boil. Add the clams, cover the pot and steam for about five minutes until the clams open. Reduce the heat and stir in the half-and-half. Do not return to a boil or the half-and-half will curdle. Serve in bowls with cocktail forks and crusty bread for dipping. Note: Mussels can be used in place of clams for a different flavor.

Serves 2

STEAMER CLAM PASTA SALAD

$^1/_2$ package (8 ounces) small shell macaroni
3 tablespoons olive oil (divided use)
3 large pressed cloves garlic
4 large sliced mushrooms
1 cup cooked steamer clams cut in two pieces
$^1/_2$ package frozen spinach, thawed and squeezed dry
20 halved green olives
$^1/_2$ cup pimientoed yellow bell pepper (Pg. 156)
$^1/_2$ can drained and chopped anchovies
1 chopped green onion
6 leaves Romaine lettuce, rib removed and chopped
    Juice from one lemon
1   teaspoon freshly ground black pepper
1 teaspoon salt

Cook the shell macaroni al dente (about 8 minutes), drain and mix with 1 tablespoon of the olive oil. Set aside to cool. Place the remaining olive oil in a sauce pan over medium heat and sauté the garlic and mushrooms until the mushrooms are limp (about three minutes). Pour the contents of the sauce pan on the pasta. Add the remaining ingredients and toss to combine. Chill in the refrigerator before serving.

Makes 4 servings.

CLAMS VERACRUZ STYLE

This is a favorite dish when we visit Mexico. Despite the number of ingredients it is easy to make and wonderfully satisfying.

    3   tablespoons butter
    1   chopped white onion
    4   finely chopped garlic cloves
  1/2   cup water
    2   large chopped tomatoes
   10   green olives, pitted and chopped
    2   seeded and diced jalapeño chili peppers
  3/4   cup seeded and diced green bell pepper
    1   teaspoon dried oregano
    1   teaspoon rosemary leaves
    2   tablespoons fresh chopped cilantro
        Juice from 1 lime
    2   bay leaves
    1   teaspoon red pepper flakes (optional)
  1/2   teaspoon salt
   20   Manila clams or cherrystones in the shell

Sauté the onion in the butter over medium heat for 5 minutes, add garlic and cook for another minute. Mix in the remaining ingredients, less the clams, cover and simmer over low heat for 15 minutes. Stir occasionally. Turn up the heat until the mixture begins to boil and add the clams. Cover the pot, reduce the heat and steam the clams for five minutes until the clams are open. Discard clams that have not opened, remove the bay leaves and serve in bowls with a side order of hot corn tortillas and a Caesar salad.

Serves 2

CRABS

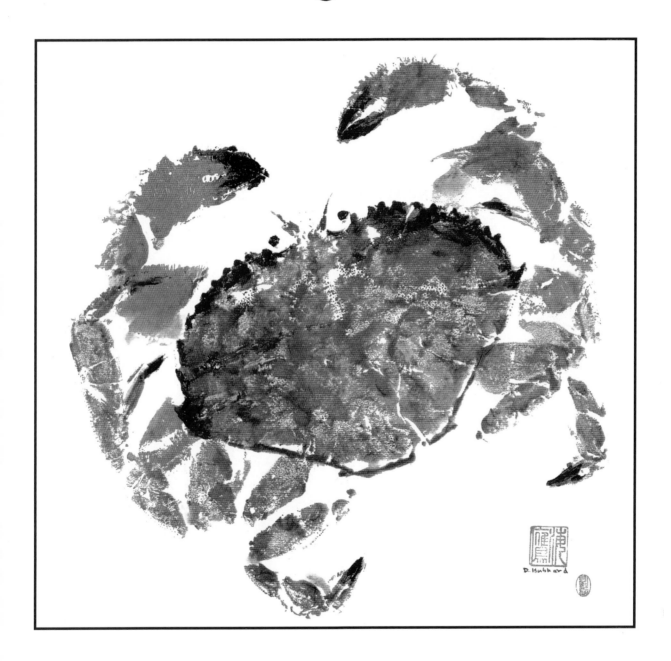

Overleaf:

The Western Rock Crab

CRABS

RECIPES IN THIS SECTION

Most of my experience has been with the blue crab of Eastern waters, portrayed on the cover. They used to be the terror of the mud flats when we went clamming. They were fast on the bite, and they could travel rapidly using two specially adapted flattened swimming legs. When you were bitten by the blue crab you knew you had been bitten. It was not rare for the larger ones to bite clear through a finger. One experience like that was enough to make you treat the blues with the utmost respect.

In Long Island Sound we used to catch these crabs with wire nets with four hinged sides that dropped down when the net was sent to the bottom. The net was baited with dead fish and if crabs were around it was not unusual to catch them fairly rapidly. We used a different technique in Jacksonville, Florida, when I was stationed there. The St. Johns River was full of blue crabs. There we tied chicken necks to strings and dropped them into the water below the pier. The crabs would find the necks, begin to eat and then hang on with one or both claws while we gently lifted them to the surface. We could easily net them because they were intent on eating. The St. Johns river yielded some really immense crabs. I remember one which measured 18 inches from claw tip to claw tip. Now that is a *big* crab.

For the crab novice, the standard way to pick up a live crab (if you don't have tongs) is to hold them by the two hindmost legs. The claws may be snapping out front, but you will be safe. If the crab is heavy, or if one or both rear legs are missing then again approach from the rear, placing your fingers beneath and your thumb on top of the body. Gently hold the crab down (a foot works) and then reach in from the back with your fingers centered between the back legs. Be careful! Don't let your fingers project too far forward since the crab can bend his claws down and inward to a limited degree and nip you.

Four of the best known crabs in America are the blue crab, the rock crab, the Pacific Coast Dungeness crab and the Alaskan King Crab. You may be able to buy the first three alive, while King Crab is usually sold in the form of cooked legs. The meat from all of them can be used interchangeably in crab recipes. Just as a matter of information, I recently cleaned three rock crabs that had a total weight of 2 pounds, 3 ounces in the shell. The three yielded $^3/_4$ of a pound of meat. You can also purchase "imitation crab" (surumi) which is nothing but a white fish named pollock which has been netted at sea and usually processed aboard a factory ship. The fish's firm white meat is given a tint of red color and some crab flavoring, then frozen. This imitation crab meat can be used in most of the crab recipes in this section.

BOILED CRABS

> **4 quarts of water**
> **2 tablespoons salt.**
> **4 live crabs**

Add the salt to the water and bring to a boil. Quickly drop in the live crabs, cover and return the water to a boil. Reduce heat and simmer for 10 minutes. The crabs will turn bright red when cooked. Drain and cool before cleaning and extracting the meat.

For **SPICED CRAB** add a packet of crab boil spices (Pg. 152) to the water before boiling, then follow the cooking directions above. The boiled spiced crab has a distinctly different flavor than plain boiled crab and is better used in crab cocktails than in some of the other recipes which have their own flavorings.

CLEANING

To clean a cooked crab, begin by breaking off the claws and legs from the body. Crack the claws with a mallet. Do this gently to avoid pounding shell into the meat. Remove the claw meat with a pick. It helps to take the smaller hinged part of the claw and bend it backwards until it detaches from the larger section. Very often a good portion of meat will come out with the cartilage. To clean the legs, crack them, twist them and either squeeze out or dig out the meat.

To extract the meat from the crab body, invert the shell and break off the "V" shaped "apron" which is hinged at the base. This apron is narrow on male crabs and large on females who use it to cover the egg mass when it is developing. With the apron off, pry the top shell away from the bottom and discard. The lower half of the body will still have the "face" of the crab attached. Break this off and discard as well. You will now have the inner crab body. There will be soft whitish gills on both sides which you must remove and dispose of. Scoop out the soft viscera in the center and rinse off the body so that the cartilage is clean, then break the body into two halves. On smaller crabs I do this by placing my thumb down in the center and bending the two halves toward the middle. Large crabs may be too hard to break. Take a chef's knife, lay it on the center line and give it a whack with a mallet.

With a sharp knife cut the cartilage sideways just above the leg sockets. This gives you a top and bottom portion. The meat will now be exposed and can be removed by twisting and pulling apart the segmented areas and by digging with a nut pick. The same process is used with the inner lobster body.

It is almost impossible to clean a crab without small bits of the shell and cartilage mixing in with the meat. Before using the meat in any recipe carefully feel through it to find and remove these hard pieces. One of the easiest ways to do this is to spread the cleaned meat out on a cutting board and gently press your fingers down into it. This will usually locate any hard shell pieces. Cartilage is harder to find because it is flat. Use a knife edge held almost sideways to push under the meat and turn it over. Watch carefully for broad opaque items which will be the cartilage. Despite all these precautions still remind your guests that small hard shell or cartilage pieces may be present.

CRAB COCKTAIL

This is a favorite appetizer in many restaurants and a choice item to enjoy at "Happy Hour" with a martini or a glass of chilled white wine.

$^1/_2$ cup chipped ice
$^1/_2$ cup shredded crab meat
 2 tablespoons seafood cocktail sauce (Pg. 157)
 1 tablespoon chopped cilantro or parsley
 1 lemon or lime wedge

This cocktail is best prepared in a special crab or shrimp/icer combination dish. The chipped ice is placed in the lower half and the crab meat is placed in an upper container which nestles down into the ice. Heap the crab meat in the upper dish and drop on a dollop of cocktail sauce. Top with cilantro or parsley as a garnish. Place the lemon or lime wedge alongside for optional use. If you do not have a combination dish, simply mound the crab on a small plate with the cocktail sauce and the citrus wedge alongside. Oyster Crackers or toast points add a nice touch.

1 serving

CRAB SALAD

  1   cup shredded crab meat
  1   finely chopped green onion
$^1/_4$ cup chopped celery
$^1/_4$ cup avocado cut into $^1/_2$ inch chunks
  3   tablespoons mayonnaise
  1   teaspoon coarse ground pepper
      Sprinkle of garlic powder
  2   chilled lettuce leaves
  2   lemon wedges
  2   generous sprigs of fresh parsley

Mix the first seven ingredients together and let the flavors blend in the refrigerator for at least one hour. Serve on chilled lettuce leaves. Pierce the lemon wedges with salad forks and lay on the serving dishes. Garnish with parsley.

Serves 2

CRAB TACO

  1   corn tortilla
  2   tablespoons finely shredded red or green cabbage
  1   tablespoon chopped green onion
  1   tablespoon chopped tomato
  1   tablespoon chopped cilantro
  2   tablespoons shredded crab meat
  1   tablespoon prepared mild salsa
  1   tablespoon sour cream or guacamole sauce (Pg. 153)

Heat the tortilla in a frying pan turning once or twice. Spread the cabbage, onion, tomato and cilantro across the center. Distribute the crab on top. Cover with salsa. Fold the tortilla sides together over the filling to form a pocket. Top with sour cream or guacamole sauce and serve.

Makes 1 taco

CRAB AND SPINACH SPREAD OR PASTA TOPPING

  1   cup cooked spinach
  1   cup shredded crab meat
$^1/_4$ cup feta cheese
$^1/_2$ cup prepared Ranch dressing
$^1/_4$ cup pimientoed red pepper (Pg. 156)
  1   teaspoon paprika

Squeeze the spinach dry and chop finely. Add the shredded crab. Crumble in the feta cheese and remaining ingredients. Mix well. You can chill this and serve it as a spread on crackers or toast, or you can heat it and use it as a topping on hot pasta.

Serves 2

CRAB AND CAPER SAUCE ON TOAST

    Caper sauce to cover (Pg. 151)
1 **slice toasted white bread**
1 $^1/_2$ **tablespoons cooked and shredded crab meat**

Spread warm caper sauce evenly over the toasted bread and cover with crab meat. Serve with a green salad and chilled white wine for a light lunch.

Serves 1

CRAB CASSEROLE

8 **ounces ($^1/_2$ package) small macaroni**
$^3/_4$ **cup whole milk**
8 **ounces cooked and shredded crab meat**
$^1/_4$ **cup chopped parsley**
$^1/_2$ **teaspoon dried thyme**
1 **teaspoon garlic powder**
$^1/_2$ **teaspoon coarse ground black pepper**
1 **teaspoon salt**
3 **tablespoons grated mild Cheddar cheese**
$^1/_2$ **cup plain bread crumbs**
2 **tablespoons melted lemon butter sauce (Pg. 153)**

Heat oven to 350 degrees

Cook the macaroni for about seven minutes. Remove from the heat while still firm. Drain and place in a mixing bowl. Add the milk and give it a stir to coat the pasta. Mix in the crab, parsley, thyme, garlic powder, pepper and salt. Stir well to evenly distribute the ingredients. Pour into a greased casserole dish and cover with the cheddar cheese and seasoned bread crumbs. Drizzle the lemon butter over the crumbs. Bake uncovered at 350 degrees for 45 minutes until the cheese is melted and the bread crumbs are slightly browned. Serve with a green salad.

Serves 4

CRAB CAKES

$^1/_2$ pound cooked and shredded crab meat
2 tablespoons finely chopped green onions
$^1/_2$ teaspoon garlic powder
2 beaten eggs
$^1/_4$ teaspoon coarse ground pepper
1 tablespoon cream sherry
3 drops Jalapeno Tabasco Sauce
$^1/_3$ cup Italian style bread crumbs
$^1/_3$ cup uncooked oatmeal
Salt to taste

For deep fat frying, heat the oil to 375 degrees

Mix the crab with the other ingredients. Form the mixture into small flattened cakes (about 2 inches in diameter) and drop them, two at a time, into the heated oil. Let each pair of cakes cook about one minute until golden brown. Remove the cooked cakes from the oil and place on absorbent paper to drain. Add the second pair to the preheated oil and repeat the procedure until all the cakes are cooked. Serve with a lemon wedge and with tartar, ketchup or sea food cocktail sauce according to preference. Minced clam meat can be substituted for the crab to make clam cakes.

Makes four cakes.

CRAB ENCHILADAS

A Mexican enchilada is simply a tortilla that has been softened by frying then filled with a sauce of some sort, rolled and baked. Because the sauce can be changed easily and dramatically, the enchilada is a versatile and exciting party dish. In this case we use a crab sauce as the inspiration. If you add the red pepper flakes be cautious, don't overpower the delicate crab flavor.

$^1/_4$ cup chopped onion
3 finely chopped cloves garlic
2 tablespoons olive oil
1 (8 ounce) can tomato sauce
1 teaspoon red pepper flakes (optional)
$^1/_4$ cup finely diced red bell pepper
$^1/_2$ teaspoon dried oregano
1 teaspoon salt
$^1/_2$ cup water
$^1/_2$ cup cooked and shredded crab meat
$^1/_2$ cup canola oil
4 (8 inch) corn tortillas
4 tablespoons grated mozzarella or Monterey jack cheese
$^1/_2$ cup sour cream

Heat oven to 400 degrees

Briefly sauté the onion and garlic in the olive oil then add the tomato sauce, red pepper flakes, the diced red bell pepper, oregano, salt and water. Bring to a boil and then simmer for ten minutes. During the last minute add the cooked crab and mix well to distribute.

Heat the canola oil in a small skillet until hot. Using tongs, dip each tortilla in the heated oil for several seconds until soft and heated through. Drain on absorbent paper.

Place a heaping tablespoon of the crab sauce in the center of each tortilla, roll and place side by side, seam side down, in an oven-proof dish. Top with the remaining sauce and grate on the mozzarella cheese. Bake in a 400 degree oven for 10 minutes until the cheese is melted. Remove from the oven, spoon sour cream on each enchilada and serve. Makes 4 enchiladas

SCALLOPED CRAB

- 1 tablespoon butter
- 2 teaspoons flour
- $^1/_4$ cup half-and-half
- 1 tablespoon cream sherry
- 1 cup cooked and shredded crab meat
- $^1/_2$ cup cooked, drained and chopped spinach
- 1 chopped green onion
- 2 finely diced cloves garlic
- 1 teaspoon chopped capers
- 2 dashes Tabasco (optional)
- 1 teaspoon lemon or lime juice
- $^1/_2$ cup crushed saltine crackers
- 2 tablespoons butter in $^1/_4$ inch cubes

Heat oven to 350 degrees.

In a small pan melt the butter and combine with the flour to make a roux. Add the half-and-half and sherry and stir over low heat until the mix thickens slightly. Carefully sift through the crab to remove any shell or cartilage, then combine with the sauce and add the spinach, onion, garlic, capers, Tabasco and citrus juice. Mix well and spoon into two ramekins. Cover with the crushed saltines and dot evenly with butter. Bake in a 350 degree oven for 20 minutes. Serve hot with green vegetable and salad.

Serves 2

SOFT SHELLED CRAB

In order to grow, a crab must periodically shed its shell and create a new larger one. Crabs which are caught during this shedding period have soft shells. After cleaning, the entire crab can be cooked and eaten. Most soft shelled crabs have been caught commercially, usually in the Chesapeake Bay, and reach the market frozen and already prepared. If you are fortunate enough to be able to catch your own softies, the cleaning process is as follows: Lay the crab on a cutting board and with a sharp knife cut away the face of the crab just behind the eyes. Turn the crab over, fold back the triangular apron and remove. Lift the points of the shell and remove all the soft matter including the gills, and viscera. Rinse the crab and chill or freeze until use.

- 3 cups canola oil
- $1/4$ cup seasoned bread crumbs
- $1/4$ cup flour
- 4 prepared soft shell crabs
- 2 beaten eggs
   Salt to taste
- 4 slices fresh sour dough bread
- 2 lemon wedges

Heat the oil to 375 degrees in a deep pot.

Combine and mix the bread crumbs and flour. Dip the crabs in the egg mixture, drain for a moment and then roll them in the combined bread crumb/flour mix to coat well. Fry in the hot oil until a uniform light brown (about 3 minutes). Be careful not to overcook. Remove from the oil and drain on paper towels. Lightly salt if desired. Serve as a sandwich on sour dough bread with tartar sauce. You can squeeze a bit of lemon juice on the crab if desired.

Soft shelled crab can be served as a separate dish without the bread.

Serves 2

LOBSTER

Overleaf:

The American Lobster

LOBSTERS

The early New England settlers found large numbers of these tasty crustaceans in the offshore waters. They were so numerous that the northeast storms would toss them on the beach to die. The farmers along the coast would take the carcasses to their fields and plow them in for fertilizer. Today the lobster population has been greatly reduced by overfishing but wise conservation efforts are under way to protect the resource.

There are two basic kinds of lobsters sold commercially: **The Eastern American Lobster** - the kind which has two large claws. It inhabits the waters from Southern Labrador to Cape Hatteras. This is the most widely fished lobster in North America with the bulk of the catch coming from the northern part of its range (Canada and Maine). It becomes somewhat less prevalent as you move south. **The Spiny Lobster** - which has prominent sharp spines on its carapace and no large claws - is found in many locations throughout the world. It is prevalent in the United States in the waters off Florida and California.

I was introduced to the American Lobster when I was a boy living on High Island, in Long Island Sound. My brother-in-law, Bill Hesse, bought a traditional oak lobster trap (pot) at the Fulton Fish Market in Brooklyn and lugged it to High Island via the subway and bus, then a mile by wagon across the foot bridge to the island. He baited this with old dead fish and set it down in about 30 feet of water off the steep rocks in front of our bungalow. The pot was not a prolific producer (maybe one or two lobsters a week) but it was still exciting and gave me my first taste of this gourmet food. I have recently discovered that there is a sub-species of the American lobster in the Eastern Long Island Sound where my brother-in-law had his trap. This sub-species is appropriately named the "Bronx Lobster".

It was in Newport, Rhode Island, where I really came to know and appreciate this great crustacean. The Navy sent me there to the Naval War College in 1965 to take a series of courses, and I used my spare time to explore the Newport area. One happy discovery was the Lobster Pound on the waterfront down on Thames Street. Here the lobster fishermen came in with their catch and the Pound sorted all of the animals by size and weight. The sorted animals were then put in labeled salt water holding pens. Those that had a missing claw or were too big for general use were put into a holding pen which was labeled "culls". Culls, of course, were much less expensive than the one and a half to two pound lobsters which were in greatest demand. I used this "cull" bin to supply the family with lobster throughout that one year tour of duty. I quickly discovered that the meat in the large lobsters was just as tender as the meat from the smaller ones, so it was usual for me to buy the animals in the five pound and up category. (I bought one that was 13 pounds and had to cook it in sections after killing it.) The hotels also bought the large culls because they were inexpensive and could be used in a wide variety of recipes that called for lobster meat.

My introduction to the California spiny lobster had to wait until 1967, when I left the Navy and became certified to use scuba gear. One of the alternate names for this species is "rock lobster" which is derived from their tendency to seek out rocky ledges and outcroppings for concealment. They are careful to hide in deep caves or under rock arches with escape routes on both sides. This is one of the reasons why California spiny lobsters are difficult to catch. California law requires that divers catch lobsters by hand. Underwater you can almost always spot the quarry in their lair by their waving antenna, so the usual technique is to propel yourself within range with a kick of your fins, then shoot your hand forward and grab. Luckily for the spiny lobsters they can rocket back into the crevices with great swiftness, so unless you are very fast, or catch them unawares, you are apt to end up smashing your hand into the rocks and bruising your fingertips. Just as possibly, you may end up holding a pair of lobster antenna. The lobster can shed these when they are held captive by them. When I had my scuba school (Ocean Ventures) I made up a fictitious recipe called "Antenna Stew" which I handed out to beginners after their first "lobster" dive.

There is one other problem associated with hand-catching spiny lobsters - the spines themselves. A miscalculation, or the wrong type of gloves, can lead to painful wounds. I well remember the gashes I received when I caught my first spiny lobster wearing cotton garden gloves. The thin gloves were absolutely no protection. After that painful lesson I switched to heavy leather and later vinyl gloves which the spines could not penetrate, but it still took a long time before I became comfortable grabbing for lobsters.

It is interesting that the larger spiny lobsters, though fewer in numbers, are easier to catch. Lobsters walk on the bottom using their legs, but they escape by snapping their tails. This propels them backwards away from the threat. The smaller lobsters, with their light weight, can shoot along faster than a diver can pursue, but the larger 8, 9, 10 pound "bulls" move sluggishly in escape making them easier to catch.

They are also easier to spot and handicapped by having fewer caves and ledges where they fit and can hide.

BASIC LOBSTER COOKERY

There are some who say that you should kill the lobster before cooking. They recommend doing this by cutting the spinal cord between the carapace (the forward part of the body) and the tail, but I have tried this and it doesn't seem to kill them quickly. I really have no taste for the procedure. Neither do I have the temperament to steam them to death. Instead I prefer to kill lobsters quickly in boiling water, then proceed with other cooking methods, if needed.

To kill and cook by boiling, bring 3 or more quarts of water to a boil and add 2 tablespoons of salt. Plunge the lobster head first into the boiling water. This kills them almost instantly though there will be some movement for a few seconds. If you have more than one lobster cook them one at a time so that their combined movement does not push one or the other partially out of the pot. If you are just killing the lobsters to cook under the broiler, remove them after 3 minutes. If you wish to complete the cooking in boiling water leave the lobsters in the water for 5 minutes per pound. They will change color and become bright red as they cook. A $1\frac{1}{2}$ pound lobster will yield about $6\frac{1}{2}$ ounces of cooked meat.

BASIC LOBSTER EATERY

When I mentioned to my sister, Doris, that I was working on lobster recipes for this cookbook, she interrupted my conversation and asked why anyone would eat lobster in any way other than dipped in melted butter. When I explained that cookbooks require more than one recipe for each chapter, her weak "Oh!" told me that she was unconvinced. She has a point.

Though I have added other recipes, the simplest and probably the best way to eat lobster, whether boiled or broiled, is to split them, remove the chunks of meat and dip in melted butter. To get at the meat in the tail and body break off the legs and claws and set aside. The tail meat peels out easily and the meat in the forward part can be extracted with a small cocktail fork or nut pick. Look for and save the greenish liver (tomalley) and any red coral roe. Both are delicious and can be eaten by themselves. The large claws of the American lobster should be cracked and the chunky meat taken out. The small legs can be broken in pieces and the meat either sucked out or pulled/pushed out with a nut pick. You can dip the pieces into melted butter directly or sprinkle with lemon juice beforehand.

BROILED LOBSTER

  1 medium lobster
$^1/_2$ stick butter, melted
  1 lemon wedge
     Salt and freshly ground black pepper

After the lobster has been killed by the short boiling period, split the lobster carcass down the middle with a sharp heavy knife and, if needed, a mallet. Crack the claws but let them remain attached to the body. Lay the two halves on a broiler pan. Remove the stomach, which is a small pocket in the forward part of the carapace, and the intestinal vein, which runs from the stomach back to the end of the tail. Brush the meat with melted butter and place about 4 inches below the flame of the broiler. Cook for 12 to 15 minutes, basting periodically with butter. The meat should be lightly browned when done. Serve the halves with additional melted butter and a lemon wedge. Salt and pepper as desired.

Serves 1 or 2 depending on appetite and size of the lobster

LOBSTER WITH ARTICHOKE HEARTS OVER LINGUINE

$^1/_2$ pound linguine
  1 tablespoon olive oil
$1^1/_2$ tablespoons butter
  2 pressed cloves garlic
  1 cup cooked and chopped lobster meat
$^1/_2$ cup chopped marinated artichoke hearts
  5 chopped black olives
$^1/_2$ cup half-and-half
     Freshly grated Parmesan cheese

Cook linguine until al dente. Drain, toss with 1 tablespoon of olive oil and keep warm. Melt the butter in a sauce pan and lightly sauté the garlic. Add the lobster, artichoke hearts, olives and half-and-half. Heat and stir until the liquid bubbles. Spoon the sauce over the linguine. Grate Parmesan cheese on top. Serve with a green salad and a dry white wine.

Serves 2

LOBSTER / AVOCADO SALAD

  8 ounces small shell noodles cooked, drained and cooled
  3 tablespoons olive oil
  1 cup cooked and chopped lobster meat
$^1/_2$ ripe avocado, chopped into $^1/_2$ inch pieces
  1 stalk finely chopped celery
  1 tablespoon chopped pimientoed red pepper (Pg.156)
  2 tablespoons finely chopped red onion
  1 teaspoon grated lime zest
     Juice from one lime

1 teaspoon garlic powder
Salt and freshly ground black pepper to taste
Combine all ingredients and chill before serving.

Serves 2

LOBSTER, GARLIC, MUSHROOM SALAD

$^1/_2$ pound fusilli or similar small pasta
6 tablespoons melted butter (divided use)
1 cup cooked and chopped lobster meat
4 large chopped mushrooms
4 finely chopped cloves garlic
   Salt and pepper

Cook the pasta as directed, drain, pour on one third of the butter, add the lobster and mix well. Set aside. Sauté the garlic and mushrooms in the remaining butter until the mushrooms are limp. Mix into the pasta. Salt and pepper to taste. Chill and serve for lunch or as an appetizer before dinner.

Serves 2

LOBSTER WITH THAI CURRY SAUCE

Making lobster meat into a curry may strike you as unusual, but the flavor of the lobster comes through without any problem if the curry sauce is not too strong. This is a wonderful alternative to other lobster dishes.

$^1/_2$ cup chopped cooked lobster meat
$^1/_2$ cup coconut milk
1 tablespoon finely chopped pickled ginger
1 tablespoon chopped cilantro
1 teaspoon curry powder
1 teaspoon fish sauce (Pg. 152)
$^1/_2$ teaspoon garlic powder
$^1/_2$ green onion, finely chopped
$^1/_2$ teaspoon coarse ground pepper
1 dash Jalapeño Tabasco

Combine all ingredients. Heat and serve on rice or over slices of French or Italian bread. You can reduce the amount of curry or eliminate the Tabasco to reduce the "heat" of this recipe.

LOBSTER NEWBURG

This is essentially a sauce into which lobster has been placed. It is terrific, but you can substitute crab, scallop or even skate wings. As an interesting aside, James Beard mentions in his book, NEW FISH COOKERY, that the name derives from Wenburg, the name of an American chef who invented the dish.

>   4 tablespoons butter
>   1 tablespoon flour
>   1 cup half-and-half
>   2 beaten egg yolks
>   Dash of cayenne pepper
> $^1/_4$ teaspoon salt
>   1 cup lobster meat, cut into $^1/_2$ inch pieces
>   2 tablespoons dry sherry
>   1 teaspoon paprika

Melt the butter and blend in the flour. Stir in the half-and-half and combine to make a smooth sauce. Bring to a simmer. Add a bit of the heated sauce to the egg yolks and mix well. Add the eggs, cayenne and salt to the sauce. Finally, stir in the lobster and sherry. Serve over toast or rice, and sprinkle on the paprika. Wonderful with asparagus, a lettuce salad and chilled dry white wine.

LOBSTER THERMIDOR

From what I gather the word Thermidor could be derived from the Greek *therme* (heat) + *doron* (gift) which makes it a "heated gift". Not a bad name for any lobster dish, but especially for this one which could just as easily, but unromantically, be called stuffed lobster.

>   2 broiled and cooled lobster halves, about $^3/_4$ pound each
>   5 tablespoons butter
>   2 tablespoons chopped green onions
>   2 finely chopped cloves garlic
>   1 $^1/_2$ cups chopped mushrooms
>   1 cup unseasoned bread crumbs
>   1 teaspoon Worcestershire sauce
>   1 teaspoon Jalapeño Tabasco sauce
>   1 $^1/_2$ ounces dry sherry
>   1 cup half-and-half
>   3 beaten egg yolks
>   Salt to taste
>   Paprika
>   Freshly grated Parmesan cheese

Heat oven to 400 degrees

Cool the cooked lobsters, break off the legs and claws and remove meat from the claws, the body and the tail. Keep the body and tail parts intact. Save the legs for garnish. Chop the lobster meat into $^1/_2$ inch pieces and set aside.

Do not remove the upper half of the leg mass inside the body since these pieces are needed to retain the filling. Clean the shells and place them in a baking dish on a layer of rock salt to steady them.

Melt the butter in a sauce pan and sauté the onions and garlic for one minute. Add the mushrooms and sauté until tender (about two or three minutes). Combine all the remaining ingredients except the paprika and Parmesan cheese and add to the sautéed garlic, onions and mushrooms. Mix thoroughly and cook stirring over medium heat until thickened. If it does not thicken sufficiently add some extra bread crumbs. Remove the thickened sauce from the heat, combine with the chopped lobster and stuff the lobster shells. Heap the mixture slightly towards the center. Sprinkle with paprika and grated Parmesan cheese. Bake in the oven for ten to twelve minutes until the top is browned and the cheese is melted. Serve hot with rice or couscous, green vegetable, green salad and a chilled white wine.

Serves 2

TOMALLEY SAUCE

The "tomalley" is the liver of the lobster and appears as a grey green substance when the lobster is split in half. Carefully remove the tomalley and use it to make the spread that follows. It has a flavor reminiscent of caviar.

> **Tomalley from one lobster**
> 2 **tablespoons sour cream**
> 1 **teaspoon lemon juice**
> **Salt and pepper to taste**

Blend together and serve on crackers or toast points as an appetizer.

LOBSTER WITH MANGO AND HORSERADISH

If you want to surprise your friends with a new and interesting lobster recipe, this is it. Mango and horseradish in the proper combination enhance the flavor of lobster without being intrusive.

- 2 **tablespoons butter**
- 2 **tablespoons flour**
- 1 **cup half-and-half**
- 1 **cup of cooked chopped lobster**
- $^{1}/_{2}$ **cup mashed meat from a ripe mango**
- 1 **tablespoon prepared horseradish**
- 2 **tablespoons cream sherry**
  Salt and pepper to taste

Melt the butter in a sauce pan, stir in the flour, then mix in the half-and-half to make a white sauce. Combine the horseradish with the mashed mango. Pour the mix into the sauce pan along with the lobster chunks. Pour on the sherry and stir while the ingredients heat. Salt and pepper to taste. Serve over cooked rice with a green vegetable and garden salad. White wine accompanies.

Serves 2

LOBSTER STUFFED MUSHROOM CAPS

- 8 **large mushrooms**
- 1 **tablespoon butter**
- 2 **finely chopped garlic cloves**
- 1 **finely chopped green onion**
- $^{1}/_{2}$ **teaspoon anise seeds**
- $^{1}/_{4}$ **cup shredded lobster meat**
- 1 **recipe for mayonnaise/dill sauce (Pg. 154)**

Remove the stems from the mushrooms and save for other uses. Wipe the caps gently with a damp cloth and set aside. Melt the butter in a saucepan and lightly sauté the garlic, onion and anise seeds for one minute. Spoon the mixture into the mushroom caps then cover with the shredded lobster meat. Top with mayonnaise/dill sauce and serve as an appetizer.

Appetizers for 2 to 4

MUSSELS

D. Hubbard

Overleaf:

Maine Mussels

MUSSELS

RECIPES IN THIS SECTION

I mentioned in the introduction that as a youngster I spent 5 months of the year living on a Bronx island in Long Island Sound. What I did not mention was that there were mussels growing in profusion all over the rocks at the tide line. They were there, but we only used them for bait. Not so the Italian immigrants who passed by in their rented rowboats. They would pry baskets of these blue mollusks off the rocks and row off to feast at home. It was not until I was in Europe in 1950 that I had a chance to sample these versatile shellfish. I could only laugh when I thought of all those years when I ignored this bounty in my own watery back yard. That has all changed. I reside in Southern California and there are large mussel beds, both here and in Baja, free for the taking.

For those who don't live by the sea, mussels can be purchased in most places in the United States and Canada. New Zealand exports their Green Mussels both in fresh and frozen form, and mussels are also grown commercially in the United States and shipped nationwide by truck, train and air. As with all seafood, the fresher the better, so it is wise to ask the grocer when the shellfish arrive at the store and buy them then.

While it is true that mussels can be gathered at many locations along both the Atlantic and Pacific coasts, it is important to be cautious! Mussels are among the most efficient filter feeders, and contaminants, either man-made or natural can accumulate in the meat. They are particularly susceptible to the "red tide" organisms which bloom periodically during the warmer months. Check with your Fisheries or Public Health people before gathering and consuming local mussels.

Mussels cling to the rocks with byssus threads. These are thin strong tendrils which are secreted by the mollusk at its base. These threads form a "beard" which must be removed before cooking. Do this by grasping the beard and pulling it toward the pointed end until it breaks loose. As an aside, I read in an oceanographic magazine some years ago that the Golden Fleece of ancient times was made of bright yellow byssus threads woven into fabric.

If you gather fresh mussels you may find that there is sand accumulated in the meat. To rid the mussels of the sand soak them for a few hours in salted fresh water to which you have added a cup of cornmeal. This works with other shellfish as well.

Mussels should be well scrubbed and examined to be certain that they have tightly closed shells. They often relax the adductor muscles after harvesting so it is not unusual for the shells to part slightly in transit. Any that appear to be gaping should be sharply rapped against the side of the sink to see if they can be shocked into closing. Rapping them is the attention getter they need. If the mussel begins closing, this indicates that the animal is alive and can be cooked and eaten. They need not close fully to pass this test. Discard any that show no reaction and remain gaped open, and discard any with cracked or broken shells. If you are not going to cook the mussels soon after purchase, put them in the refrigerator in a bowl to allow them to breath, and cover them with some ice. Drain the bowl every day so that the mussels do not soak in fresh water. If they are submerged for too long they will suffocate because they need oxygen.

After cooking, the mussels should open. Once again, discard any that do not. These mussels were probably dead before cooking and sometimes may be full of mud or sand.

As a general rule there are about 20 - 25 commercially grown mussels to the pound.

Remember, when you serve mussels in the shell you will need an extra bowl for the discarded shells. Dipping crusty bread through a pile of empty shells cuts down on the enjoyment.

MUSSELS MARINIERE

- $1/2$ **large onion finely diced**
- 3 **finely chopped cloves garlic**
- 2 **tablespoons butter**
- 2 **tablespoons olive oil**
- $1/4$ **cup dry vermouth**

Juice $^1/_2$ lemon or lime
1   cup water if mussels are in shells. $^1/_4$ cup if meat only.
$^1/_4$ cup chopped parsley or cilantro
    Freshly ground pepper to taste
1   pound mussel meats or 2 pounds mussels in shells
Note: If mussel meats are large you may wish to cut them in half.

Sauté onion and garlic in melted butter/olive oil mixture until onions are translucent. Transfer to a deep pan. Add vermouth, lemon/lime juice, water, parsley/cilantro, pepper and mussels. Turn up the heat and steam the mussels until open (about 5 minutes). Give the mussels a stir about half way through the cooking process. If using mussels which have been previously cooked and extracted from the shells, turn up the heat enough to warm well. Heat for an additional 2 - 3 minutes. Serve in bowls with the liquid. Use crusty French or Italian bread for dipping the broth. A green salad and a chilled white wine complete the meal.

Serves 2

MUSSELS MEXICANA

The west coast of the Baja Peninsula is home to vast beds of large mussels. Deep kitchen middens attest to the fact that the early native population dined on these tasty mollusks long before the arrival of the white man. Understandably mussels are still a favored part of coastal Mexican cuisine. The following recipe is based on many enjoyable meals I have had south of the border.

$^1/_2$ pound cooked mussel meats. If large cut in half
2   tablespoons olive oil
2   finely chopped cloves garlic
$^1/_2$ cup chopped onion
$^1/_2$ cup chopped green bell pepper
2   seeded and finely chopped jalapeño peppers
$^1/_2$ cup garbanzo beans
4   sliced marinated artichoke hearts
4   fresh chopped leaves basil
1   (8 ounce) can tomato sauce
$^1/_2$ cup water
2   tablespoons tequila con gusano
    Juice of $^1/_2$ lemon
1   teaspoon salt

Combine all ingredients in a large pan and when you add the tequila toss in the gusano for good measure. Bring to a boil then reduce heat to a simmer. Serve with refried beans topped with melted cheddar cheese, hot corn tortillas and a Caesar salad.

Serves 2

MUSSELS NEWBURG

This is essentially the same sauce as we use for lobster newburg, but we have altered it by adding sour cream and cilantro. Mussels have a strong enough flavor to be able to handle the complimentary cilantro/sour cream tastes.

- **4 tablespoons butter**
- **1 tablespoon flour**
- **$^1/_2$ cup half-and-half**
- **$^1/_4$ cup sour cream**
- **2 beaten egg yolks**
- **2 tablespoons cream sherry**
- **1 pound cooked mussel meats, cut in half if large**
- **$^1/_2$ cup chopped cilantro**
- **Dash cayenne**
- **Salt**

Melt the butter, add the flour and blend. Stir in the half-and-half and sour cream and heat until the sauce begins to thicken. Combine a bit of the hot sauce with the egg yolks and add the mixture to the pan. Stir in the sherry, cooked mussels, cilantro and cayenne and bring to a simmer. Salt to taste. Serve over rice with a green vegetable and crisp salad. Compliment with a chilled dry white wine.

Serves 4

MUSSEL SAUCE WITH LINGUINI, SPINACH AND SOUR CREAM

- **2 tablespoons butter**
- **3 chopped green onions**
- **2 finely diced cloves garlic**
- **3 large chopped mushrooms**
- **$^1/_2$ cup cooked spinach, squeezed dry and chopped**
- **1 teaspoon coarse ground pepper**
- **$^1/_2$ cup sour cream**
- **12 medium mussels, steamed and removed from shells**
- **8 ounces linguini**

Melt the butter in a medium skillet and sauté the onions, garlic and mushrooms until soft. Add the spinach and pepper. Mix in the sour cream and mussels and stir until the mussel meats are heated through and the sour cream is hot. Cook the linguini al dente, drain and serve with the sauce.

Serves 2

MUSSEL PASTA SAUCE WITH TOMATOES

$^1/_2$ package (8 ounces) small shell macaroni or spaghetti
3   tablespoons olive oil (divided use)
$^1/_2$ cup chopped onion
3   finely chopped cloves garlic
1   cup whole canned peeled tomatoes, crushed
$^1/_4$ cup red wine
$^1/_2$ teaspoon sugar
$^1/_2$ teaspoon basil
$^1/_2$ teaspoon coarse ground black pepper
    Salt to taste
$1\,^1/_2$ pounds mussels in their shells
$^1/_2$ cup chopped parsley

Prepare the pasta as directed, drain and mix in 1 tablespoon olive oil. Keep warm.

Sauté onions and garlic in remaining olive oil. Stir in the crushed tomatoes with the tomato liquid and wine. Add the sugar, basil, pepper and salt and bring to a boil. Add the mussels and return to a boil. Stir occasionally until the mussels open (about 5 minutes). Remove from heat and drop in parsley. Place cooked pasta into large soup bowls. Spoon mussels and sauce over the pasta and serve with lots of napkins, green salad and red wine.

Serves 2

STUFFED MUSSELS

1   pound mussels in shell
$^1/_4$ cup finely chopped green onion
$^1/_4$ cup finely chopped mushroom
3   tablespoons butter
1   cup seasoned bread crumbs
2   tablespoons finely chopped parsley or cilantro
    Salt and pepper to taste
    Freshly grated Parmesan cheese

Steam the mussels until open and remove the meat. Remove the upper shell and replace the meat in the bottom half. Sauté the green onion and mushrooms in butter until the mushrooms are limp, then mix with the bread crumbs, parsley/cilantro, salt and pepper. Spoon some of the mixture on each of the mussels and cover with a bit of Parmesan cheese. Place under a broiler until slightly browned. Serve hot as an hors d'oeuvre.

Serves 2

MUSSELS PILAF WITH PINE NUTS

$^1/_2$ cup water
$^1/_2$ cup dry vermouth
  2 pounds mussels in their shells
  3 chopped green onions
  2 finely diced cloves garlic
  2 tablespoons olive oil,
    Chicken broth or bottled clam juice to make 2 cups of liquid
  1 cup long grain rice
$^1/_4$ cup pine nuts
$^1/_4$ cup chopped parsley
$^1/_4$ cup chopped red pimientos (Pg. 156)
$^1/_2$ cup crumbled Feta cheese

Combine the water and wine and steam the mussels in the liquid until the mussels are open (about 5 minutes). Set aside to cool then remove the meat. Reserve the cooking liquid. Sauté the green onion and garlic in olive oil for two minutes until the garlic is cooked. Measure the mussel liquid and add sufficient chicken broth or clam juice to make two cups. Add to the sauce pan with the rice and onion/garlic mix. Stir to distribute, then bring to a boil. Cover and cook over low heat for 15 minutes or until the rice is cooked. Add the mussel meats, pine nuts, parsley and pimientos to the cooked rice and mix well. Place on serving dishes and top with the crumbled Feta cheese. Fresh cooked spinach is a nice compliment.

Serves 2

MUSSEL SOUP

  2 pounds mussels in the shell
$^1/_2$ cup white wine
$^1/_2$ cup water
  4 tablespoons ($^1/_2$ stick) butter
$^1/_2$ cup chopped red onion
  5 finely chopped garlic cloves
  1 (28 ounce) can of whole peeled tomatoes and canned juices
$^1/_2$ teaspoon oregano
$^1/_2$ teaspoon basil
$^1/_4$ teaspoon fennel
  1 teaspoon sugar
    Salt and pepper to taste

Steam mussels in the combined wine and water mixture until the mussels are open (about 5 minutes). Set aside and reserve the liquid. Melt the butter in a sauce pan and sauté the onions and garlic for one minute. Add the remaining ingredients. Pierce and crush the tomatoes before adding. Cover and simmer for 30 minutes to blend the flavors. You can add $^3/_4$ cup bottled clam juice to the soup to increase its volume if you wish. Place the mussels and soup in large soup bowls. Serve with garlic bread and salad.

Makes a hearty soup for 2

Alternatives: You can substitute red wine for the white and clams, shrimp, scallops or calamari for the meat. The final flavor will differ with each substitution but don't hesitate to try the alternates.

TOMATO-FREE MUSSEL SPAGHETTI SAUCE

    3 **tablespoons butter**
    1 **finely chopped small onion**
    2 **finely chopped or pressed cloves garlic**
    2 **pounds fresh mussels in the shell**
  $^1/_4$ **cup dry vermouth**
  $^1/_4$ **cup of water**
  $^1/_2$ **pound spaghetti or linguini**
      Parmesan cheese

Melt the butter in a skillet and sauté the onion and garlic for one minute. Steam the mussels in the combined wine water mixture until open (about 5 minutes). Save the liquid for other uses and remove the mussel meat. Cook the pasta as directed on the package, drain and mix in the butter sauce, then add the mussel meats. Sprinkle with Parmesan cheese and serve with a chilled green salad.

Pasta for 2

MUSSELS A L'ESCARGOT

If you have ever enjoyed snails in garlic butter you will understand the appeal of this dish. Canned snails are expensive, and live snails (yes, from your garden - they are edible) are trouble to prepare. Mussels, on the other hand, are readily available and comparatively inexpensive. The flavor is slightly different, but still magnificent.

    2 **pounds mussels in shells**
    1 **stick ($^1/_4$ pound) butter**
    3 **pressed cloves of garlic**
    2 **tablespoons minced fresh parsley**
    1 **tablespoon lemon juice**
      Salt and pepper to taste

Pre-heat oven to 450 degrees.

Steam the mussels until open, remove the meat when cool and discard the upper half of the shell. Cream the butter and mix with the remaining ingredients. Place each mussel meat in a half shell and spoon a dollop of the butter mixture on top. Bake in the oven for a few minutes until the butter is bubbling hot. Serve with cocktail picks or small forks.

Serves 4

MUSSELS WRAPPED IN BACON

> 2 pounds mussels in shells or 1 pound mussel meat
> Sliced bacon as required

Steam the mussels until open and remove the meat. Wrap each mussel meat in a piece of bacon and pin in place with a toothpick. Broil, turning often until the bacon is done. This usually takes about 10 to 15 minutes, depending on the broiler and closeness to the flame. Drain quickly on absorbent paper. Serve on toothpicks with a bit of chopped parsley as a garnish.

Makes hors d'oeuvres for 4

MUSSELS IN CREAM SAUCE

> 2 pounds fresh mussels in the shell
> 1 large clove garlic, pressed into the cooking pot
> 1 cup water
> $^1/_2$ cup dry vermouth
> 2 egg yolks
> $^1/_2$ cup half-and-half
> 1 tablespoon butter
> 1 tablespoon cream sherry
> Salt and pepper to taste

Place the mussels and pressed garlic in the combined water and vermouth and steam about 5 minutes until mussels are open. Let cool slightly and remove the meat from the shells. Reserve the broth. Beat the egg yolks, combine with the half-and-half and cook in a sauce pan until the mixture thickens slightly, then stir in the sherry and four tablespoons of the mussel broth. Add the mussels, reheat and serve over rice or pasta. Complete the meal with asparagus, a green salad and chilled white wine.

Serves 2

MUSSELS STEAMED IN DARK BEER

While preparing this book I wrote to a good friend in Holland, Elly de Koster, who is an etcher of some note and who specializes in ex- libris, the art of the bookplate. I sent her my collection of mussel recipes and mentioned that as a native of Holland, where mussels are grown commercially and eaten in abundance, she might have some recommendations. The following four recipes were forwarded in her next correspondence. I especially enjoyed her method of timing the cooking by allowing the steam to raise the pan lid. Good idea.

> 1 $^1/_2$ cups water
> 1 bottle (12 fluid ounces) dark Dutch beer
> 2 $^1/_2$ pounds mussels in the shell
> 1 sliced large onion
> 1 leek, green part, chopped
> 2 chopped carrots

1 large chopped stalk celery
¹/₂ cup chopped parsley
2 bay leaves
  Salt and pepper to taste

Pour the water, beer and other ingredients in a deep pan. The mussels should rise about half way up the pan sides. Cover and bring to a boil. The boiling mixture will begin to raise the pot lid at which time raise the lid to release the steam, close again and cook for one or two more minutes. The mussels will have opened by this time, releasing their juices into the beer mixture. Serve in individual bowls with crusty garlic bread and ice cold Dutch beer.

Serves 2

MUSSELS SAUTÉED IN BUTTER

4 tablespoons butter
¹/₂ cup chopped onion
3 finely chopped cloves garlic
1 cup mussel meat from the above beer recipe

Melt the butter in a sauce pan, add the onions and garlic and sauté until the onions are translucent. Add the mussel meat and cook stirring until the meat begins to brown slightly. Serve with boiled potatoes, sautéed yellow squash and chilled white wine.

Serves 2

BAKED MUSSELS

¹/₂ cup general purpose flour
¹/₂ cup bread crumbs
¹/₂ teaspoon garlic powder
  Salt and pepper to taste
2 tablespoons melted butter
1 cup meat from the beer steamed mussels
¹/₂ cup chopped parsley
2 chopped green onions

Mix the flour, bread crumbs, garlic powder, salt and pepper. Melt the butter. Dip the mussels in butter, then in the flour/bread crumb mixture. Bake in the oven for 20 minutes at 375 degrees. Serve hot on toast with a garnish of parsley and chopped green onions, or with mashed potatoes and a green salad.

Serves 2

PICKLED MUSSELS

$^1/_2$ cup white vinegar
2 tablespoons sugar
$^3/_4$ cup sliced red onion
1 chopped clove of garlic
1 bay leaf
  Salt and pepper to taste
2 cups steamed mussels removed from the shell

Combine the first six ingredients and bring to a boil in a stainless steel pot or in a microwave proof glass bowl. Mix in the mussels and refrigerate overnight. Serve as a light lunch with a green salad. The pickled mussels can be kept in the refrigerator for up to three weeks.

Serves 4 for lunch

OCTOPUS

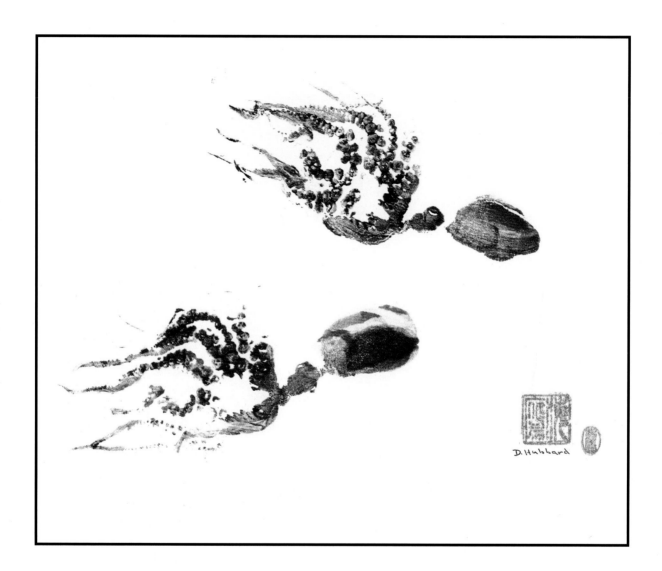

Overleaf:

Two Small Octopi

OCTOPUS

RECIPES IN THIS SECTION

Though cooked octopus is a very fine food, many people find it unnerving. This may be because of the fictional stories and movies which portray the animal as the villain, and it almost certainly has to do with the animal's appearance. Eight legs with prominent suckers and a soft bulbous head with kind-of shifty eyes does not equate to a cuddly kitten. Nevertheless octopi are not dangerous. In fact they are rather shy animals and hard to find when you are diving or searching along the shore at low tide. Octopi hide in caves and crevices during the day and generally only venture forth after dark to search for food. You can sometimes spot their lairs by the piles of small shells stacked outside, but it takes a keen, knowing eye to do this. However, there are times when you will surprise an octopus in shallow water roaming outside its den during the day. If you are fast they are relatively easy to catch. They have a small parrot-like beak concealed directly amidships beneath the head, and they can nip if sufficiently provoked. They rarely do.

Octopi are classified as mollusks and have a mild flavor akin to the muscular parts of a clam to whom they are related. The meat is white and tender when properly prepared and has texture and chewing qualities similar to lobster. Fresh and cooked octopus can be found in many ethnic Mediterranean and Asian food markets. There are some octopus varieties in the ocean that are huge, but the usual store offerings rarely exceed eight pounds (pretty big) You will also find octopus as small as an ounce or less (10 to 25 to the pound). If you wish to cook the larger variety choose one in the 2 to 4 pound size. This will provide plenty of meat and the size is more manageable. Both the large and the small (which is a species not a baby) can be prepared and used in a variety of exciting and tasty recipes, some of which are offered here.

PREPARATION

When you have purchased uncooked octopus, rinse under cold running water and then inspect to determine whether the head cavity needs cleaning. Larger animals are usually cleaned when you buy them, but the very small versions are probably not. If you must clean these little critters, simply slit open the head cavity from the vent tube and remove the easily detachable interior matter. Then split the tentacles between the shortest two and remove the hard beak and its surrounding muscle pack. Rinse. You will notice that very little material has been removed overall. This is one of the benefits of octopus. A pound of purchased octopus is very nearly a pound of edible food after cleaning. Compare this with the waste matter when you buy lobsters, clams, crabs, shrimp or fish.

Uncooked or undercooked octopus can be tough stuff, so proper preparation is essential but not difficult. Cooking simply involves pre-boiling the meat in salted water for half an hour, then allowing it to cool in the liquid. The proper technique for placing larger octopus in boiling water is to hold them by the head and dip them in the water for a few seconds, withdraw and air cool for about 30 seconds. Dip again and repeat the air cooling. Finally, place the octopus in the water and simmer for the prescribed cooking time. The meat will be more tender if this procedure is followed since the protein is modified gradually and does not toughen. A Spanish gentleman explained this to me when I purchased my first large octopus in an Asian food store. That was truly an international event. The addition of a bay leaf or two adds to the flavor. Test before cooling to see whether a fork penetrates easily. If not, add another five or ten minutes to the cooking, but do not overdue. Too much cooking results in meat that is too soft.

If you are preparing a larger octopus cut the head off at the tentacle tops after cooking, then cut off the portion of the head which has the eyes. Feed this to the kitties or bury next to a favorite plant to promote growth. The tiny tentacle tips can be added to the fertilizer application since they are too small to provide much nutrition but do add to the tangle. The remaining animal can be cut into chunks for use in the recipes. The skin and suckers do not have to be removed. The head usually has the toughest meat, so it should be diced most finely or even ground up if it is to be used in a sauce or chowder. With the very small animals you can use them in your recipe as is, or separate the head and tentacles and use the latter, which curl into a flower- like pattern as an edible decorative touch. There is no need to remove the eye portion of the head from the small variety before eating.

CURRIED OCTOPUS WITH SWEET AND SOUR SAUCE

This makes a fine oriental style sauce with a variety of uses.

- **1 pound cooked octopus**
- **¹/₂ bottle sweet and sour sauce**
- **3 tablespoons chopped pickled ginger (Asian stores) or fresh grated ginger.**
- **4 teaspoons curry powder**
- **3 tablespoons chopped chutney.**

The octopus can be finely chopped or used in bite-sized chunks. Put in a bowl and add all the other ingredients except the chutney. Heat to a simmer and allow the mixture to marinate overnight

Reheat and serve over rice with chutney, vegetable and salad.

Serves 2

OCTOPUS SPAGHETTI SAUCE

This is one of many Italian-style spaghetti sauces that can be enhanced with the addition of octopus meat. The octopus contributes both protein and its own mild octopus flavor.

- **3 tablespoons olive oil**
- **1 cup coarsely chopped onion**
- **3 finely chopped cloves garlic**
- **1 pound cooked chopped octopus**
- **1 (14.5 ounce) can peeled, cut up, tomatoes**
- **1 (6 ounce) can tomato paste**
- **1 teaspoon sugar**
- **1 teaspoon dried oregano**
- **¹/₂ teaspoon dried basil**
- **¹/₄ teaspoon fennel seeds**
- **¹/₄ teaspoon dried thyme**
- **1 bay leaf**
  Freshly grated Parmesan cheese
- **¹/₂ cup chopped fresh parsley**

Heat oil, add onions and garlic and sauté until the onions are opaque. Add remaining ingredients and simmer for 15 minutes. If time permits allow the mixture to sit for several hours to blend before reheating. Serve hot over spaghetti noodles with grated Parmesan cheese. Garnish with parsley. Garlic bread and a bottle of red wine can make this dish memorable.

Makes sauce for 2 servings

OCTOPUS COCKTAIL

This recipe substitutes finely chopped octopus for crab to make an individual seafood cocktail. It is simple to make and flavorful.

  2 **tablespoons seafood cocktail sauce (Pg. 157)**
$1/2$ **cup finely diced, cooked and chilled octopus meat**
    Lemon or lime wedge
    Oyster crackers

Place the seafood cocktail sauce in the top half of an ice filled shrimp/icer combination dish. Add the chopped octopus and squeeze on lemon or lime juice as desired. Serve as an appetizer with oyster crackers.

Cocktail for 1

OCTOPUS HORS D'OEUVRES WITH MELTED BUTTER

As mentioned in the introduction, octopus are classified as mollusks so it is not surprising that their meat tastes very much like the meat of clams. This dish capitalizes on this close flavor relationship and makes an interesting exotic seafood hors d'oeuvre.

  2 **tablespoons butter**
  2 **finely chopped garlic cloves**
    Juice $1/2$ lime
$1/4$ **cup chopped cilantro**
  1 **pound small cooked octopus or 1 pound large octopus, cooked and cut into $3/4$ inch pieces**

Melt the butter and lightly sauté the garlic. Add lime juice and chopped cilantro. Place individual small octopus or large octopus chunks on toothpicks. The meat can be either warm or cold. Dip individual pieces in the butter/garlic sauce and eat as you would small steamed clams or mussels.

Makes hors d'oeuvres for 8

MEXICAN STYLE OCTOPUS

I first tasted this interesting recipe in a small Mexican restaurant in Ensenada, Baja California. This was a restaurant where the native folk ate, so the varied cooking smells and authentic Mexican decor added to the excitement. It was here that I discovered that octopus can be genuinely tender.

  1 **pound chopped up pre-cooked octopus**
$1/3$ **cup water**
  1 **(14.5 ounce) can whole tomatoes broken up with juice**
  3 **finely chopped cloves garlic**
  1 **chopped medium onion**
  1 **chopped medium tomato**
  1 **finely sliced stalk celery**
$1/2$ **cup seeded, finely diced, green bell pepper**

1   seeded and finely chopped Jalapeño pepper
10 pitted, lightly chopped ripe olives
2   tablespoons olive or vegetable oil
1   teaspoon dried oregano
$1/2$ teaspoon dried thyme
1   Bay leaf
$1/2$ cup chopped cilantro
3   drops Tabasco sauce
    Salt to taste

Combine all ingredients, cover and simmer for an hour over low heat. Stir periodically. If too dry add additional water or red wine. Serve over rice with refried beans and hot flour tortillas. Cold Mexican beer (cervesa) adds to the authenticity.

Serves 4

Note: it is rare to finish all of the above at one sitting. I usually combine the main dish with the leftover rice and beans and have a cold feast for lunch the next day.

COLD OCTOPUS SALAD

For anyone who enjoys a mildly spicy cold seafood salad.

1   cup cooked octopus chopped into $1/2$ inch pieces
3   cups cold cooked pasta (sea shells/fusilli, etc.)
$1/4$ cup olive oil
1   tablespoon dried basil
$1/4$ teaspoon garlic powder
1   chopped medium tomato
3   chopped green onions
1   thinly sliced stalk celery
3   tablespoons Mexican salsa
3   dashes tabasco
$1/3$ cup chopped marinated artichoke hearts
    Salt and pepper

Toss and mix all the ingredients and chill for one hour in the refrigerator. Enjoy with a glass of chilled dry white wine.

Salads for 2

OCTOPUS WITH MUSHROOMS

This makes a delicious, satisfying and easily prepared meal.

- **1 pound small octopus**
- **2 finely chopped cloves garlic**
- **4 sliced large mushrooms**
- **2 tablespoons olive oil**
- **$^{1}/_{4}$ cup cream sherry**
- **1 (10 $^{3}/_{4}$ ounce) can Cream of Mushroom Soup**
- **Coarse ground black pepper to taste**
- **Freshly grated Parmesan cheese**
- **$^{1}/_{4}$ cup chopped fresh parsley**

Chop the octopus into small pieces. Sauté the garlic and mushrooms in oil until the mushrooms are limp. Combine octopus, mushrooms, garlic, wine, cream of mushroom soup and pepper in a sauce pan and heat until warmed through. Serve over pasta or rice with freshly grated Parmesan cheese and a garnish of parsley.

Serves 2

SMALL OCTOPUS IN TOMATO/WINE SAUCE

- **1 chopped medium onion**
- **4 finely chopped cloves garlic**
- **2 tablespoons olive oil**
- **1 pound cooked small octopus**
- **1 (14.5 ounce) can crushed whole tomatoes**
- **1 (8 ounce) can tomato sauce**
- **$^{1}/_{2}$ cup dry red wine.**
- **$^{1}/_{2}$ cup chopped cilantro**
- **2 teaspoons dried Oregano**
- **3 drops Tabasco**
- **1 teaspoon sugar**
- **Salt and pepper to taste**

Sauté onion and garlic in olive oil until onion is translucent. Add all other ingredients and simmer over low heat for 20 minutes to blend flavors. Serve with rice, salad, green vegetable and dry red wine.

Serves 4

OCTOPUS AND CLAMS WITH VEGETABLES

The combined flavors of this dish served over a neutral base, like rice or noodles, make an unforgettable meal for a cold winter day.

> 2 tablespoons olive oil
> 1 chopped medium onion
> 3 finely chopped cloves garlic
> 1 cored and chopped firm apple
> 2 chopped fresh tomatoes
> 3 thinly sliced carrots
> 1 thinly sliced stalk celery
> 1 cup chopped parsley
> 1 tablespoon dried thyme
> 1 teaspoon dried oregano
> $^1/_4$ teaspoon rosemary
>   Salt and pepper to taste
> 1 pound chopped, cooked octopus
> $^3/_4$ cup dry white wine or vermouth

Lightly sauté all vegetables and herbs in olive oil. Combine with precooked octopus and wine. Simmer uncovered for thirty minutes over medium heat. Serve hot as an entrée or over linguine, egg noodles or rice, with salad and garlic bread.

Serves 2

SKEWERED OCTOPUS ON THE GRILL

The round cross-section of octopus tentacles makes them a perfect candidate for grilling. The recipe requires that you use the tentacles from an octopus that weighs in at about 2 pounds or more. Try this for an unusual and appetizing way to serve this versatile meat.

> 2 cups cooked octopus tentacles sliced into $^3/_4$ inch rounds
> $^1/_2$ an onion cut into one inch squares
> 6 (10 inch) bamboo skewers soaked in water
> $^1/_2$ cup sweet and sour sauce (Pg. 158)

Light the barbecue to obtain a nice bed of fiery coals.

Thread the tentacle rounds and onion squares on the bamboo skewers leaving about an inch of exposed bamboo on each end. Place the prepared skewers in a high sided dish and cover with the sweet-and-sour sauce. Marinate for 15 - 30 minutes while the barbecue heats up. When the coals are ready, raise the grill to medium height and place the skewered meats side by side in the center. Turn often and brush on the marinade as the kebabs cook. Remove and serve when the meat has been heated through and the marinade has congealed on the outside.

Shish kebabs for 2

OCTOPUS WITH CURRY AND GINGER

This recipe is the height of simplicity, yet tasty and satisfying.

- **2 tablespoons butter**
- **4 finely chopped cloves garlic**
- **1 tablespoon freshly grated ginger**
- **1 teaspoon curry powder**
- **1 cup cooked, cross-sliced octopus tentacles**
- **Salt and pepper to taste**

Melt the butter in a sauce pan and sauté the garlic for 30 seconds over medium heat. Drop in the ginger and curry powder and mix well to blend. Add the octopus and heat through while stirring. Salt and pepper to taste. Serve with rice and a green vegetable, or serve on toothpicks as an hors d'oeuvre. You can vary the spiciness of this mixture by changing the proportions of curry and ginger.

Note: this combination is also very effectively used with other seafood, most notably shrimp or mussels.

Serves 2 for a meal or 4 for hors d'oeuvres

OYSTERS

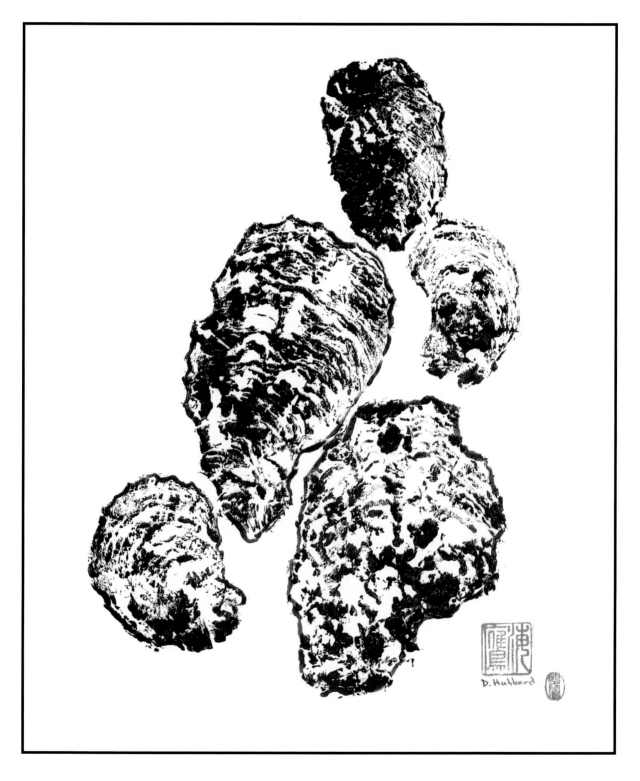

D. Hubbard

Overleaf:
Eastern and Western Oysters

OYSTERS

RECIPES IN THIS SECTION

Oysters were not a part of my Bronx childhood. I am certain that they were very much available in New York; they were just not on the paths that I traveled. My introduction to this tasty and versatile shellfish had to wait until I was several years in the Navy and half way through flight training.

During flight training we were not allowed to have vehicles, so all travel was by public transportation. I was on liberty in Pensacola, Florida and waiting for the bus to return to the Naval Air Station. I had just missed the previous bus and had to wait more than half an hour for the next. It was 10 P.M., and I was mighty hungry. By good fortune there was a small cafe next to the bus stop and heavenly odors were drifting out the door. The temptation was too much. I followed the smell in to the counter and took a seat. The cook was frying oysters and the sniff test alone told me that they would be good. I ordered a dozen followed by twelve more and thus began my lifelong attachment to this succulent seafood.

Fresh oysters both in and out of the shell are now available throughout the country thanks to improved refrigeration and fast transportation. Shucked oysters normally come in 8 or 10 ounce glass or plastic jars which are time dated. These oysters are usually stronger in flavor than the fresh product. Oysters in the shell are found in good seafood markets and the type of oyster will vary depending on location. The large Western oysters come in from San Francisco and points north, while the smaller "Eastern" oysters are shipped from beds located in the bays and sounds of the East and South.

There used to be an unwritten prohibition about eating oysters during the the late Spring and Summer months. Summer is oyster breeding time and the oysters are less plump and more watery during this period. The saying was, "Oysters 'R' in season", which referred to the months of the year which had an 'R' in them. May, June, July and August do not have an "R" while all the rest do. This rule is now rarely followed and you can buy and consume oysters all year round throughout the United States and Canada

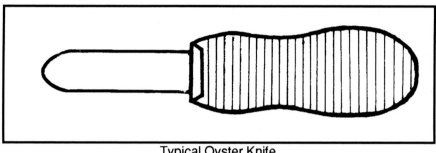

Typical Oyster Knife

SHUCKING AN OYSTER

For those who have never shucked oysters it pays to learn the technique. There is nothing quite like a fresh oyster served right out of the shell. Begin by scrubbing the oysters with a stiff brush to remove any mud, sand, seaweed or other debris that might be clinging to the outer shell. Secondly, please buy yourself an oyster knife. They are not expensive, but they greatly assist in the shucking operation. An oyster knife is a small knife with a short, stiff symmetrically shaped pointed blade. The blade measures roughly two and a half inches long by a half inch wide. The handle is fairly large in diameter and the blade stiff to assist in the pushing, twisting, prying motion necessary to open the shell. Because you are using a knife it is a good idea to wear a heavy glove on the oyster holding hand. Heavy leather, Kevlar or chain mail fisherman's gloves are what most oyster shucker wear.

Place the oyster on a cutting board with the flat (bottom) side up and hold it in place with your spare hand. Even if you *are* wearing gloves do *not* position the holding hand so that the blade will hit you if it slips. The knife may still penetrate a glove. Place the tip of the blade just alongside the hinge on the pointed end, and along the seam where the two shell halves meet. With firm but gentle pressure and a slight rocking motion on the knife, force the blade between the shells and then twist. Some shell splinters may be dislodged during this process, but eventually the knife point will pop the hinge. Now your knife can enter the oyster. Slide the blade along the flat half of the shell to sever the adductor muscle, then discard this shell half. The oyster will now be laying in the deeper upper half of the shell with most of its juices intact. Check that no shell pieces remain in the meat before eating or using the oyster in your recipe.

By the way, if you don't have or can't find an oyster knife try using a screw driver. They are sturdy enough to allow the necessary twisting motion. The problem is, you will have to have a paring knife or something similar to reach inside the oyster and sever the adductor muscle

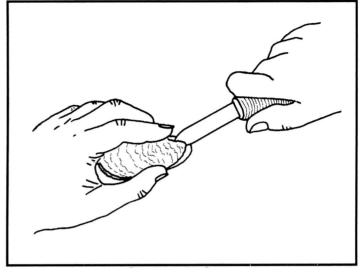

Shucking An Oyster

OYSTERS ON THE HALF SHELL

For each person

Shuck 6 oysters using the technique described above. Place the shells on a bed of crushed ice. Serve with a lemon wedge and freshly ground pepper. Some prefer a touch of seafood cocktail sauce with a dash of prepared horseradish. While it is alright to pick out the meat with a small cocktail fork, it is easier and just as correct to pick up the shell and tilt the oyster into your mouth in one motion. This way you also get the juices which add to the flavor. Serve with oyster crackers.

OYSTERS ON THE HALF SHELL WITH PIMIENTO AND BACON

6 shucked Eastern oysters
Wedge of lemon
6 ($1/2$ inch) pieces of pimientoed sweet red peppers (Pg. 156)
1 strip of bacon cooked crisp and broken into six pieces

Place the shucked oysters on the larger of the two shell halves and place on a dish of crushed ice for stability when serving. Squeeze some fresh lemon juice on each oyster, lay on a slice of pimiento and a piece of bacon. Pick up the entire shell and tip back into your mouth so that you eat the oyster with the entire contents of the shell including the juice. Wonderful as an appetizer with sips of ice cold Danish akvavit.

Note: In Denmark the bottle of akvavit is kept chilled and served in special akvavit shot glasses which are stowed in the freezer with the liquor. The glasses have thick bases to maintain the chill after the liquor has been poured.

OYSTER OMELET 1

    2 tablespoons butter
    1 tablespoon finely diced onion
    2 cloves pressed garlic
    1 tablespoon chopped green bell pepper
    2 beaten eggs
    2 shucked fresh oysters
      Salt and pepper to taste
      Sprig of parsley

Melt the butter in a sauce pan and lightly sauté the onions, garlic and green pepper. Add the oysters and cook until the edges of the oysters begin to curl. Turn over once during the cooking. Move the oysters and the other solids to the center of the pan. Pour in the beaten egg and let it flow around the other ingredients. Keep the pan moving while the eggs cook and set. Fold the egg over the oysters on both sides and slide the omelet on to a serving dish. Serve with corn bread muffins and garnish with a sprig of parsley.

1 serving

OYSTER OMELET 2

    1 tablespoon olive oil
 1 $^1/_2$ tablespoons chopped green bell pepper
 1 $^1/_2$ tablespoons chopped green onion
    1 pressed clove garlic
    4 canned, smoked oysters
    2 beaten eggs,
      Salt and pepper to taste
    2 tablespoons low fat Ranch dressing

Heat the olive oil over medium heat in a suitable sauce pan. Add the bell pepper, onion, garlic and oysters and stir fry until the pepper and onions are slightly limp and the garlic cooked, about 3 minutes. Pour in the egg mixture and distribute the vegetables evenly. Allow the eggs to cook and thicken while moving the pan to prevent sticking. The egg mixture should slide about as you move the pan. When the egg mixture is firm use a spatula to fold one edge two thirds of the way towards the center, then repeat with the other edge. Slide the omelet onto a serving dish, sprinkle with salt and pepper and top with the Ranch dressing.

Makes 1 omelet

OYSTERS WITH BRANDY

This makes a nice wake-up breakfast, especially if you flambé the brandy on the oysters just as they are served. Even if the brandy does not "flambé", and there is a good failure rate in that game, you have still had a good laugh and the brandy flavor remains.

1 tablespoon butter
1 tablespoon finely diced onion
1 pressed clove garlic
2 freshly shucked oysters and their juices
1 ¹/₂ tablespoons brandy or cognac

Melt the butter in a small saucepan and sauté the onions and garlic over medium heat until the onions are opaque and the garlic cooked (about 1 minute). Add the oysters and their juices and cook them until the edges of the oysters begin to curl. Turn over once during the process. Place the cooked oysters in a heated ramekin. Meanwhile put the brandy in a small sauce pan and heat to warm it. This should only take 10 or 15 seconds. If the brandy ignites on the stove cover it with a pan to smother the flame and quickly pour over the heated oysters. Whatever you do, don't boil the brandy as this removes the alcohol which is the flaming ingredient. Pour over the hot oysters and light with a match. When the flame extinguishes itself sit down and enjoy.

Serves 1

DEEP FRIED OYSTERS

12 shucked oysters
2 beaten eggs
2 cups of finely crushed soda crackers
   Canola oil for cooking

Heat the canola oil in a deep fat fryer to 375 degrees.

Place the shucked oysters in the beaten egg and swirl them around to coat all sides. Remove the oysters from the egg mix one at a time, drain for a second or two, then roll in the cracker crumbs. Set the crumb covered oysters aside on plastic wrap or waxed paper. When all of the oysters have been prepared place them, three or four at a time on a slotted spoon and lower them into the heated oil. If you have a splatter screen now is the time to use it to cover the cook pot. Deep frying oysters causes a lot of minor under-oil explosions which toss the oil quite a distance and make clean up difficult. If you do not have a splatter screen deflect the flying oil with a piece of cardboard or other suitable material. The oysters will cook rapidly and should be done in 30 seconds or less. Use the slotted spoon to scoop them out of the oil and lay them on a folded newspaper covered by a paper towel to drain. Repeat with the remaining oysters, but always allow the oil to return to the 375 degree temperature between sets. Serve the oysters with lemon wedge, salt and pepper

1 or 2 servings depending on the appetite.

OYSTER BISQUE

This is a classic oyster stew that can be prepared in many ways. This is the method I like best.

- 4 tablespoons butter
- 1 small finely chopped leek or green onion
- 2 finely chopped cloves garlic
- 10 plump shucked oysters, juices saved
- $1/4$ cup cooked spinach
- 3 cups half-and-half
  Salt and coarse ground pepper to taste
- 2 tablespoons flour
  Dash of nutmeg

Melt the butter in a sauce pan and lightly sauté the leek and garlic. Place the oysters in a blender. Add the sautéed mixture, the cooked spinach, the half-and-half, salt and pepper. Purée for 10 seconds. Return mixture to the pan and heat until simmering. Gradually stir in the flour while cooking until the mixture thickens slightly. Serve with a sprinkle of nutmeg on top and add croutons or oyster crackers.

Serves 4 as a first course or 2 as a lunch.

OYSTERS LASAGNA

- 1 package lasagna noodles
- 2 dozen fresh oysters in the shell
- 2 tablespoons dry sherry
- $1/2$ cup sliced black olives
- 4 large sliced mushrooms
- $1/2$ cup chopped parsley
- 3 slices bacon cooked firm and crumbled
  Garlic powder
  Coarse ground pepper
- 2 cups Ricotta cheese
- 1 cup shredded mozzarella cheese
- 1 cup Italian style seasoned bread crumbs
- 2 tablespoons melted butter

Heat oven to 350 degrees

Cook the lasagna noodles as directed on the package, drain and rinse in cold water.

Shuck the oysters and carefully check for shell bits. Discard the juice. Cut the meat into bite sized pieces. Lightly oil a square pyrex baking dish and place a layer of lasagna noodles on the bottom. Cover with half the oyster meat, a tablespoon of sherry, sliced olives, mushrooms, parsley, bacon chips, a sprinkle of garlic powder and pepper. Dot with a layer of ricotta cheese. Add another layer of noodles and repeat the sequence. Cover with a layer of noodles, sprinkle with the mozzarella cheese and seasoned bread crumbs in that order and drizzle on the melted butter. Bake covered in a 350 degree oven for 30 minutes. Uncover and bake for an additional 10 minutes to brown the bread crumbs.

Serves 4

OYSTERS WITH SPINACH AND RANCH DRESSING

- **6** **fresh oysters in the shell**
- **2** **tablespoons water**
- **2** **tablespoons Marsala wine**
- **$1/4$** **cup cooked spinach, squeezed dry, chopped and heated**
  Ranch dressing
- **1** **strip crisp cooked bacon**
  Freshly grated Parmesan cheese

Shuck oysters and reserve their juices and the large half of the shell. Poach the oysters in their juices with the water and Marsala wine for about 1 $1/2$ minutes until the edges of the oysters curl. Position and level the reserved oyster shells on a bed of rock salt and add a teaspoon of the heated chopped spinach. Place a poached oyster on the spinach, add a dollop of the ranch dressing, a piece of cooked bacon and top with grated Parmesan. Broil the oysters for about a minute to melt the cheese and serve.

Serves 1

OYSTERS IN COCONUT MILK WITH CURRY

- **1** **jar (8 fl. oz.) or six fresh oysters**
- **2** **ounces coconut milk**
- **2** **tablespoons chopped green onions**
- **$1/2$** **teaspoon garlic powder**
- **2** **ounces Thai Green Curry Sauce (Asian markets)**
- **1** **tablespoon preserved ginger - chopped**

Poach the oysters in their own juice with the coconut milk, green onions and garlic powder until the edges of the oysters begin to curl. Remove from the heat, drain all but about one tablespoon of the liquid. Add the curry sauce and preserved ginger. Mix well and reheat until simmering. Serve with rice and a green salad.

Serves 2

OYSTERS ROCKEFELLER

This is a New Orleans recipe which originally used absinthe as a main flavoring ingredient. Absinthe is now illegal in the United States and most other countries, but its unique flavor is essential in this dish. Some chefs use Pernod or anisette liqueur as a substitute, but I use ground anise seeds. These seeds still impart the necessary flavor, but are more apt to be part of the home cook's inventory.

- 1 cup cooked spinach
- 2 tablespoons melted butter
- 3 finely diced green onions
- 2 pressed cloves garlic
- 2 dashes Jalapeño Tabasco sauce
- 1 teaspoon ground anise seeds
- $1/2$ teaspoon paprika
- 2 tablespoons water
- $1/2$ cup fine crushed soda crackers
- 12 shucked oysters on the half shell

Heat oven to 450 degrees

Squeeze the spinach dry and finely chop. Melt the butter in a sauce pan and lightly sauté the onions and garlic. Add the diced spinach, Jalapeño sauce, anise, paprika, water and crushed soda crackers. Mix well. Put the oysters in the deepest half of their shells and place the shells on a layer of rock salt in an oven proof dish to balance. Place a teaspoon of the spinach mixture on each oyster and bake at 450 degrees for 10 minutes or until the topping has browned. Serve hot with a lemon wedge.

Makes 2 servings

OYSTER SHOOTERS

This is a favorite "Happy Hour" snack in many California restaurants and bars.

- 1 oyster shucked with juices
- 1 tablespoon seafood cocktail sauce (Pg. 159)
- $1/4$ teaspoon prepared horseradish
- 2 drops Worcestershire sauce
- $1/2$ ounce vodka (optional)
  Wedge of lemon
  A handful of oyster crackers

The first five ingredients are combined in a large shot glass and served chilled with a cocktail fork. Lemon juice can be squeezed on if desired. The oyster is lifted out and eaten raw with sips of the liquid, or the whole may be consumed in one shot by tipping up the glass. Enjoy with oyster crackers.

Makes 1 shooter

SCALLOPED OYSTERS

2 (8 ounce) jars small oysters with liquor
2 cups coarsely crushed soda crackers
2 cups seasoned bread crumbs
$^1/_4$ pound (one stick) butter
2 tablespoons medium dry sherry
   Coarsely ground black pepper

Heat oven to 325 degrees

In an oven-proof loaf dish place a layer of oysters with oyster liquor. Cover with a layer of crumbled soda crackers and seasoned bread crumbs. Dot with butter and a sprinkle of pepper. Repeat with two additional layers. Dribble on sherry. Cover with a final layer of crushed soda crackers. Bake in a 325 degree oven for 45 minutes and serve hot with peas and a green salad.

Serves 2

SMOKED OYSTER PASTA SALAD

6 ounces ($^1/_2$ package) rotelle pasta
1 tablespoon olive oil
1 can (3 $^3/_4$ ounce) smoked oysters, drained and oysters halved
6 chopped cherry tomatoes
2 tablespoons chopped green onions
2 tablespoons chopped cucumber
2 tablespoons pimientoed sweet red pepper (Pg. 156)
2 tablespoons parsley pesto (Pg. 156)
1 tablespoon fresh lemon juice
1 tablespoon lemon zest
1 teaspoon oregano
$^1/_2$ teaspoon garlic powder
1 tablespoon tarragon vinegar
1 - 2 dashes Tabasco sauce (optional)

Cook the pasta al dente, drain and mix in the olive oil to coat the surface and prevent sticking. Add all of the remaining ingredients and mix well. Refrigerate overnight to allow the flavors to blend.

Makes pasta salad for 4

OYSTER STEW

1   (8 ounce) jar fresh oysters - cut in chunks
$^1/_4$ cup water
$^1/_4$ cup sherry or dry vermouth
2   cups half-and-half
1   tablespoon butter
$^1/_4$ cup chopped parsley
     Sprinkle of garlic powder
     Salt and pepper to taste

Put oysters and oyster liquor in combined water and sherry and simmer until the edges of the oysters curl. Add half-and-half and heat until hot but not boiling. Add the butter, parsley and seasonings. Reheat to melt the butter. Place in soup bowls and serve with warm French or Italian bread plus salad. A dry white wine is called for here.

2 servings

SMOKED OYSTERS WRAPPED IN BACON

1   can (3 $^3/_4$ ounce) smoked oysters
4   slices raw bacon cut into thirds
     Lemon juice
     Toothpicks soaked in water

Open the canned oysters and pour off the oil. There will be about 12 oysters in the can. Wrap each oyster in a piece of bacon and hold in place with a wetted toothpick. Place the wrapped oysters under the broiler, turning each oyster so that the bacon browns nicely on each side. Remove the oysters from the pan and drain briefly on a folded paper towel. Place on a serving dish and squeeze on a bit of lemon juice. Serve as an hors d'oeuvre.

Makes about 12 to 14 pieces

SCALLOPS

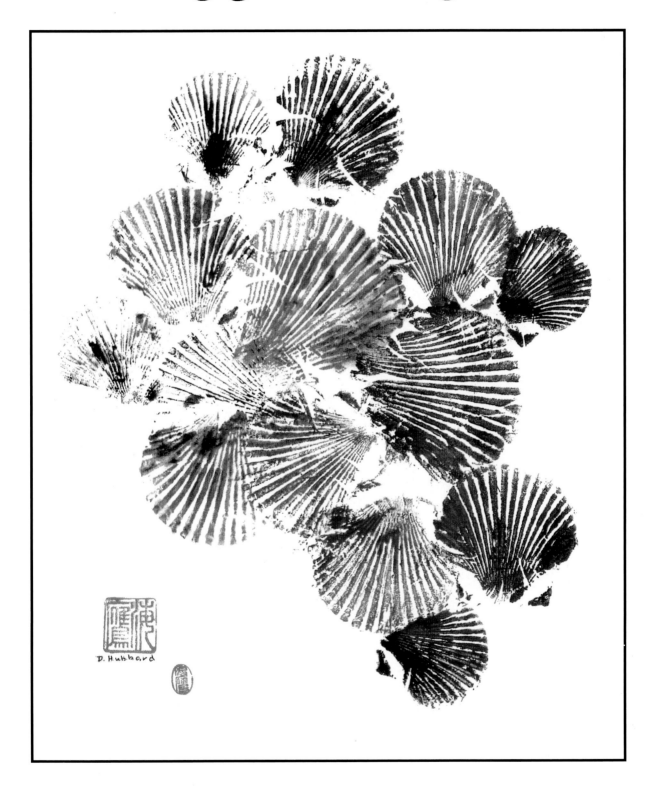

D. Hubbard

Overleaf:

A Medley of Scallops

SCALLOPS

RECIPES IN THIS SECTION

Most cookbooks describe scallops as free moving mollusks with the ability to propel themselves along the bottom by rapidly opening and closing their shells. This is true of *most* scallops, but it is certainly not true of the rock scallops which inhabit the cold waters off the West Coast. True to their name, rock scallops settle down on a rocky surface during the larval stage and permanently attach themselves. As it grows the shell conforms to the shape of the rock, and the top attracts marine growth of all kinds. As a consequence the scallop is protected from most predators, but the price it pays is immobility. When I had my diving school we used to search the rocky outcroppings for these morsels, which were usually quite large. When we found one we would go in with our knives and cut the large adductor mussel away from the shell, then take it to the surface to eat raw. On one dive I was hungry and decided that it was pointless to wait until surfacing, why not eat the meat on the spot, 60 feet down? I removed the regulator from my mouth, popped in the scallop and began chewing. Unfortunately I also allowed a gulp of water to follow the scallop, and I began to cough. Terrific! It is really not good form to be coughing 60 feet below the surface. Fortunately I am reasonably under control under water so I simply forced myself to cough around and through my regulator, which by that time was safely back in my mouth. That was a good lesson. There is a time to dive and there is a time to eat scallops, and the two do not necessarily coincide.

Aside from the aforementioned rock scallop, most commercially harvested scallops fall into two categories; sea scallops and bay scallops. For basic identification, the sea scallops are large and the bay scallops are small. They taste the same and cook the same and can be used interchangeably in all scallop recipes. The exception is that for some recipes you might wish to cut the larger sea scallops down to a more workable size.

The part of the scallop that most people eat in the United States is the adductor muscle which snaps the two shell halves together. It is not commonly known in this country that the rest of the scallop is edible and can be eaten just as you might eat a whole clam or muscle. In many countries of the world this is the case. The meat is not wasted.

As with many seafoods, don't overcook. Scallops toughen with too much cooking. Since they can be eaten raw, you can see that just heating them through is sufficient. Scallops are also quite delicate, so you must be cautious about using overly strong seasonings or the flavor will be lost.

RAW SCALLOPS

As I mentioned earlier, scallops can be eaten raw. They have their own delicate flavor and a firm consistency. On one recent Baja kayaking trip I came upon a group of Mexican sea urchin fishermen who had harvested some rock scallops while underwater. They slyly handed one to me to see what I would do. Of course I promptly bit into, chewed it up and swallowed it. The fishermen were impressed. Not too many gringos will accept raw seafood and eat it. We all stood there together eating the large scallop muscles as we might eat apples. It was a wonderful adjunct to my lunch that day.

Though your chances of finding yourself on a beach being offered raw scallop by a fisherman is remote, you can still enjoy scallops raw. Squeezing a bit of lemon or lime juice on the meat adds a bit of piquancy that compliments and enhances the delicate scallop flavor.

BREAKFAST SCALLOPS

    2 tablespoons butter
    1 tablespoon chopped red onion
    $^1/_4$ pound bay scallops or quartered sea scallops
    1   lightly beaten egg
       Salt and pepper to taste

Melt the butter in a frying pan and sauté the onion until translucent. Add the scallops and any juices. Keep the scallops moving in the pan and sauté for about 2 minutes. Add the beaten egg and scramble until cooked and mixed with the onion and scallops. Salt and pepper to taste. Serve with crisp bacon and toast. Breakfast for 1.

SCALLOPS DIJONNAISE

- 2 tablespoons butter
- 2 tablespoons olive oil
- 1 pound scallops
- 4 ounces dry vermouth
- 2 ounces half-and-half
- $^1/_2$ teaspoon Dijon-style mustard
- 1 tablespoon flour blended into
- 2 tablespoons lemon juice

Melt the butter and mix with the olive oil. Sauté the scallops in the combined oils for 2 minutes. Add the vermouth, then the half-and-half and blend together with a whisk. Cook for 1 more minute. Add the Dijon mustard and the flour/lemon juice mix. Stir while heating until the mixture thickens slightly. Serve over hot rice with asparagus.

Serves 4

SCALLOPS ITALIANO

- 8 ounces flat noodles
- 2 tablespoons olive oil (divided use)
- 2 tablespoons butter
- 3 pressed cloves garlic
- 4 chopped mushrooms
- 1 tablespoon flour
- $^2/_3$ cup half-and-half
- 1 teaspoon oregano
- $^1/_2$ pound bay scallops or sea scallops quartered
- 2 tablespoons freshly grated Parmesan cheese

Cook the noodles as directed on the package, rinse quickly and toss with a bit of olive oil. Set aside. Melt the butter in a saucepan and combine with the remaining olive oil. Sauté the garlic and mushrooms in the oil until the mushrooms are soft (about 1 minute). Whisk the flour into the oil mixture then pour in the half-and-half and stir over medium heat until the sauce is slightly thickened. Add the oregano and scallops and stir until the scallops have been warmed through and slightly opaque. Pour the scallop sauce over the pasta and grate on the Parmesan cheese. Serve with garlic bread, a green salad and a chilled dry white wine.

Serves 2

SCALLOP KABOBS

Juice $^1/_2$ lemon
1 tablespoon olive oil
$^1/_2$ teaspoon garlic powder
$^1/_2$ teaspoon dry dill weed
1 pound sea scallops
10 mushroom caps
$^3/_4$ inch squares green bell pepper
$^1/_8$ inch slices leek-white parts
4 ten inch bamboo skewers soaked in water to retard burning

Combine the lemon juice with the olive oil, garlic powder and dill weed. Marinate the scallops and mushroom caps in the mixture for 20 minutes making sure that each scallop and mushroom cap is coated. Thread the scallops on the skewers alternating with the mushroom caps, green pepper squares and leek disks. Broil on the barbecue turning to insure even cooking. Brush on the marinade as the cooking progresses to keep the ingredients moist. Serve hot.

Serves 4

SCALLOPS AND LEEKS ON LINGUINE

The delicate flavor of scallops sautéed with leeks and mushrooms, and the contrasting color of the pimientoed red bell pepper make this combination an interesting seafood pasta dish.

$^1/_2$ package (8 ounces) linguine
3 tablespoons butter
1 thinly sliced leek, white part only
1 thinly sliced large mushroom
2 pressed cloves garlic
$^1/_2$ pound bay or quartered sea scallops
$^1/_4$ cup diced pimientoed red bell peppers (Pg. 156)
2 tablespoons chopped parsley (divided use)
Freshly grated Parmesan cheese
Salt and pepper

Cook the linguine as directed on package, drain and melt on one tablespoon of the butter. Set aside and keep warm.

Melt the remaining two tablespoons of butter in a sauce pan and sauté the leeks, mushrooms, and garlic until the mushrooms are soft. Add the scallops, pimientoed red peppers and half the parsley to the pan and stir-fry until the scallops whiten slightly and are heated through. Ladle the scallop mixture on the cooked linguine and top with grated Parmesan and the remaining parsley. Salt and pepper to taste.

Serves 2

SCALLOPS AND PASTA NEWBURG

Once again we use the basic Newburg sauce to bring out the delicate flavor of a favorite seafood. This time, however, we add puréed avocado to the sauce to create a new and interesting alternate taste.

- $^1/_2$ **package (8 ounces) linguine**
- 2 **teaspoons olive oil**
- 4 **tablespoons butter**
- 2 **pressed cloves garlic**
- 1 **tablespoon flour**
- 1 **cup half-and-half**
- 2 **beaten egg yolks**
   Puréed meat of one avocado
- 2 **tablespoons dry sherry**
- 1 **teaspoon paprika**
   Dash cayenne
   Salt
- $^1/_2$ **pound bay or quartered sea scallops**

Cook the linguine as directed on the package, drain, coat with olive oil, set aside and keep warm.

Melt the butter in a sauce pan, lightly sauté the garlic, then add the flour to make a paste. Whisk in the half-and-half and heat while making a smooth blend. Spoon a bit of the sauce into the beaten egg to heat it slightly, then add to the pan. Stir in the puréed avocado, the sherry, paprika, cayenne and salt, then add the scallops and heat through for a few minutes while stirring.

Serve over linguine with green salad and white wine.

Serves 2

SCALLOPS WITH ORANGE JUICE AND DILL

- **Juice from two oranges**
- $^1/_2$ **tablespoon dry dill weed**
- $^1/_2$ **pound bay or quartered sea scallops**
- 1 **tablespoon butter**
   Salt to taste
- 4 **tablespoons grated Swiss cheese**

Mix the orange juice with the dill weed and marinate the scallops for at least three hours or overnight. Melt the butter in a sauce pan, add the scallops and orange juice mixture and poach for five minutes. Transfer the scallops to two heated ramekins, salt lightly and sprinkle on the Swiss cheese. Place under the broiler for a minute or two to melt the cheese. Serve with toast and marmalade.

Serves 2 for breakfast

SCALLOP PASTA SALAD WITH AVOCADO / CREAM SAUCE

- 8 ounces small shell pasta
- 3 tablespoons olive oil
- 2 tablespoons butter
- 2 large pressed cloves garlic
- $^1/_2$ pound halved bay scallops or quartered sea scallops
- $^1/_2$ cup avocado/cream sauce (Pg. 150)
- 1 chopped medium tomato
- 1 thin sliced green onion
  Salt and freshly ground pepper

Cook the pasta as directed on the package, drain, mix in one tablespoon olive oil and let cool.

Melt the butter in a sauce pan and combine with the remaining olive oil. Sauté the garlic lightly then add the scallops. Keep the scallops and garlic moving until the scallops turn slightly opaque. Remove from the heat and let cool for a few minutes. Pour on the avocado/cream sauce and combine the scallops and sauce with the pasta. Add the tomatoes and green onion. Sprinkle with salt and pepper and mix well. Let the salad chill in the refrigerator overnight. Serve cold.

Serves 2

SCALLOP PASTA SALAD WITH TRIPLE SEC

The sweetness of the Triple Sec is offset by the lemon juice giving this dish a slight sweet/sour flavor.

- 12 ounces rotolle (or similar small) pasta
- 2 tablespoons olive oil
- 1 tablespoon butter
- 3 finely chopped large cloves garlic
- $^1/_2$ pound bay scallops or sea scallops cut into quarters
- $^1/_2$ cup seeded and chopped cucumber
- 1 chopped green onion
- 1 tablespoon chopped capers
- 2 tablespoons lemon juice
- 1 tablespoon orange zest (grated orange skin)
  Salt and pepper to taste
- 3 ounces (2 jiggers) Triple Sec

Cook the pasta according to the directions on the package, drain, rinse in cold water. Pour on the olive oil, mix well and set aside. Melt the butter in a sauce pan, add the chopped garlic and cook for one minute, stirring to prevent scorching. Add the scallops and cook for 2 minutes until scallops are opaque. Remove from heat and allow to cool. Pour the scallop mixture over the pasta. Add the remaining ingredients including the Triple Sec. Stir well to combine. Refrigerate one hour to chill and blend flavors.

4 servings

SCALLOPS WITH CURRY / SOUR CREAM SAUCE

- 2 **finely chopped cloves garlic**
- 2 **tablespoons butter**
- $^1/_2$ **pound bay or quartered sea scallops**
- $^1/_2$ **cup light curry/sour cream sauce (Pg. 152)**
  Salt and pepper to taste

Lightly sauté the garlic in the butter, add scallops and their juices. Cook for 3 minutes until the scallops are slightly opaque and heated. Serve with warmed curry/sour cream sauce on rice. Salt and pepper as desired. Garnish with sliced mushrooms, cucumber and tomato. Include a wedge of lemon.

Serves 2

COQUILLES SAINT JACQUES

This impressive sounding dish is a standby in seafood cookbooks. This is my version.

- 1 **pound bay or quartered sea scallops**
- 3 **chopped green onions**
- $^1/_2$ **cup dry vermouth**
- 4 **chopped large mushrooms**
- $^1/_2$ **cup water**
  Juice of 1 lime
- 2 **tablespoons butter**
- 2 **tablespoons general purpose flour**
- $^1/_2$ **teaspoon garlic powder**
- $^2/_3$ **cup half-and-half**
- $^1/_2$ **cup seasoned bread crumbs**
  Freshly grated Parmesan cheese

Heat oven to 400 degrees.

Combine the scallops and green onion in the dry vermouth, bring to a boil and cook for three minutes. Remove the scallops to a separate dish and save the remaining liquid. Meanwhile cook the mushrooms in half cup of water with the lime juice. Remove the mushrooms and set aside with the scallops. Pour the remaining water/lime juice mixture into the scallop cooking liquid. Melt the butter and whisk in the flour, garlic powder, then the half-and-half. Stir until smoothly blended. Mix in the scallops and mushrooms and place all in a square 8 inch oven-proof dish or individual ramekins. Grate on the Parmesan cheese and sprinkle the top with the bread crumbs. Note: if you put the cheese on last it will darken and harden. Bake in the oven until the top is browned (about 15 minutes).

Serves 6.

SCALLOPS WITH MARINATED ARTICHOKE HEARTS

   8 ounces small shell or similar pasta.
   2 tablespoons olive oil (divided use)
   2 tablespoons butter
   3 finely chopped cloves garlic
   2 chopped green onions
$^1/_2$ pound bay scallops   (or)
$^1/_2$ pound quartered sea scallops
$^1/_2$ cup sour cream
   4 quartered marinated artichoke hearts
      Salt and pepper to taste

Cook pasta as directed on package, drain and coat with one tablespoon of olive oil.

Combine the remaining olive oil and butter in a sauce pan and lightly sauté the garlic and green onions. Add the scallops and stir in the pan until opaque and cooked (about 3 minutes). Stir in the sour cream and combine with the remaining ingredients. Serve over the pasta with a green salad and chilled white wine.

Serves 2

SCALLOPS WITH RANCH DRESSING AND GREEN ONIONS

If you want a very simple but tasty scallop dish, this is it.

2 tablespoons butter
2 finely chopped cloves garlic
$^1/_2$ pound bay or quartered sea scallops
1 tablespoon lemon juice
$^1/_4$ cup Ranch salad dressing

Melt the butter in a pan and lightly sauté the garlic. Add the scallops and lemon juice and cook for 2 minutes, stirring. Add the Ranch salad dressing and cook for one more minute until heated. Serve with rice or couscous, spinach and a green salad.

Serves 2

SCALLOPS POACHED IN WINE

$^1/_2$ pound bay or quartered sea scallops
$^1/_2$ cup dry vermouth
$^1/_2$ cup curry and sour cream sauce (Pg. 152)

In a medium sauce pan bring the wine to a boil, add the scallops and cook for two or three minutes until heated through and opaque. Serve covered with curry/sour cream sauce. Parsley potatoes, asparagus with Hollandaise sauce and a green salad are perfect companions for this dish.

Serves 4

SHRIMP

D. Hubbard

Overleaf:
Dancing Shrimp

SHRIMP

RECIPES IN THIS CHAPTER

I approached writing about shrimp with happy anticipation. I have eaten shrimp in such diverse places as North Africa; Europe; Guantanamo Bay, Cuba; Baja, Mexico; all over Japan; in the Philippines, in Hong Kong and during the war, in Vietnam; and that does not even include all of the fine restaurants in the United States. Yes, this is a shell fish where possible cooking combinations are almost infinite.

Anyone who saw the movie Forrest Gump will remember the wonderful sequence when Gump's platoon mate, Bubba, recited a seemingly endless list of shrimp recipes. This is a direct quote: "Shrimp is the food of the sea. You can barbecue it, boil it, broil it, bake it, sauté it, shrimp kee bobbs, shrimp Creole, shrimp gumbo. You can pan fry, deep fry, stir fry, pineapple shrimp, lemon shrimp, coconut shrimp, pepper shrimp, shrimp soup, shrimp stew, shrimp salad, shrimp in potatoes, shrimp burgers, shrimp sandwich - that's about it." But the clever sequencing of the movie, from scene to scene, leaves you with the impression that Bubba has been going on and on about shrimp for most of the day. He must have. I did not hear him mention shrimp manicotti, shrimp cocktails, shrimp with mango, shrimp egg rolls and shrimp rémoulade, shrimp scampi, shrimp spaghetti sauce, shrimp tempura, shrimp saté and shrimp Teriyaki - which, among others, we have been pleased to add.

So when I fell to the task of formulating and testing shrimp recipes for this book, how could I resist and how could I do anything but enjoy it. As always in food preparation there were some unexpected discoveries which will add to the richness of my future cooking and possibly add a touch of surprise for you and your guests. Have fun and feel free to improvise. There are a lot of shrimp out there!

SHRIMP SHELL PURÉE

It is surprising that the shells of shrimp have a great deal of flavor of their own and can be used as a food source. In earlier times the shells were reduced using a mortar and pestle, but with the advent of electric blenders the chore of grinding the shells to an edible fineness is eliminated. Try this recipe and rejoice at the added calcium and roughage in your diet.

Shells from $1/2$ pound of shrimp
2   chopped cloves garlic
2   cups water
$1/2$ teaspoon salt
1   cup cooked rice
$1/4$ cup coconut cream (or half-and-half with $1/2$ teaspoon coconut extract)
2   teaspoons dry sherry

Boil the shrimp shells and garlic in 2 cups of salted water for five minutes. Pour the hot mixture into a blender and purée until the shells are chopped into minuscule size. Add the rice, coconut cream and sherry. Blend until the mixture is smooth. You can vary the flavor by adding spices of your own. Reheat and serve as a purée or pour over additional rice or Indonesian vegetables.
Serves 2

SHRIMP FLAVORED RICE

Here is another creative way to use the shrimp shells to transform something as common as rice into an unusual dish.

- 3 cups water
- 1 tablespoon salt
  Shells from one pound of shrimp
- 1 tablespoon teriyaki sauce (Soy sauce can be substituted)
- 1 cup of rice

Bring the salted water to a boil and add the shrimp shells. Boil gently for five minutes. Drain the water through a sieve reserving 2 cups for the rice. Dispose of the shells. Place the water, rice and teriyaki sauce in a rice cooker or pot and cook as for normal rice. Serve hot with butter.

Serves 2

SHRIMP COCKTAIL

Shrimp cocktails are a common offering in most restaurants. They are not hard to make and are a wonderful appetizer to serve special guests.

- 10 large shrimp in the shell
- $^1/_2$ cup seafood cocktail sauce (Pg. 157)
- 2 cups shaved ice
- 2 sprigs of parsley
- 2 lemon wedges

Shell and devein the shrimp but leave the tail on. Sauté as for shrimp scampi #1 (below) then chill in the refrigerator. Prepare the seafood cocktail sauce. If you are fortunate enough to have special shrimp/icer combination dishes fill the base dish with the shaved ice. Place the upper dish on the ice and fill with $^1/_4$ cup of the seafood cocktail sauce. Place 5 chilled shrimp into the sauce - large end down, tails up. Garnish with a piece of parsley and serve with a wedge of lemon.

For those who do not have shrimp/icer dishes (most of us I imagine) put the shaved ice in bowls and cover the ice with a leaf of lettuce. Symmetrically lay five shrimp on each and serve with a small ramekin containing the seafood cocktail sauce for dipping, or put a dollop of the sauce at the center of the shrimp.

Makes 2 cocktails

SHRIMP AND FENNEL SPREAD

This is an interesting spread that is low calorie, tasty and easy to prepare.

   6 **boiled and shelled medium shrimp**
  $^1/_2$ **cup plain yogurt**
  $^1/_2$ **teaspoon garlic powder**
   1 **tablespoon chopped fresh fennel flowers or 1 teaspoon crushed fennel seeds**
      Salt to taste

Chop the shrimp finely. Mix together with the remaining ingredients, chill in refrigerator for 3 hours and serve as a spread on bagels, toast or crackers.

Makes about $^3/_4$ cup of spread.

SHRIMP OMELET

Every time I look at this recipe I am reminded of breakfasts in the small Mexican village of San Felipe, in Baja. San Felipe is in the upper part of the Sea of Cortez and as we ate we could sit at our table and look out at the shrimp boats towing their nets. Later in the day we would buy freshly caught shrimp from vendors who walked the beach.

   3 **tablespoons butter (divided use)**
   5 **peeled, deveined and coarsely chopped medium shrimp**
   2 **chopped green onions**
   2 **tablespoons finely chopped seeded jalapeño pepper**
  $^1/_4$ **cup chopped fresh tomato**
   2 **chopped small mushrooms**
   1 **teaspoon dried dill weed**
   5 **chopped capers**
   4 **eggs, beaten lightly and mixed with 2 teaspoons cold water**
      Salt and pepper to taste

In an large pan with rounded sloping sides lightly sauté the shrimp, green onions, jalapeño pepper, tomato and mushrooms in 1 $^1/_2$ tablespoons of the butter until the shrimp are pink and the vegetables softened. Remove from pan, mix in the dill weed and capers, set aside and keep warm.

Melt the remaining butter in the pan over medium heat and coat the sides of the pan well. Pour in the egg/water mixture and stir to spread it well over the pan. As the egg begins to congeal, gently tip the pan from side to side lifting the edge of the forming omelet to allow the uncooked egg to run off and contact the heated surface. Periodically shake the pan to keep the egg from sticking. Distribute the cooked shrimp mixture along the center of the omelet. Using a spatula fold one-third of the cooked egg over the ingredients, then fold the other third over the first. Remove from the stove and slide the omelet on to a serving dish. Sprinkle with salt and pepper and serve with bacon, refried beans and hot corn tortillas. Bueno!

Makes 1 large omelet for 2

SHRIMP IN PLUM SAUCE

Plum sauce is a sweet sauce used in Asian cooking. Shrimp cooked this way makes an excellent appetizer or side dish.

- **1 teaspoon canola oil**
- **2 tablespoons prepared plum sauce**
- **12 peeled medium shrimp**
- **2 finely chopped cloves garlic**
  Several sprigs of cilantro

Place the canola oil and plum sauce in a sauce pan and mix well. Add the shrimp and garlic and sauté over medium heat until the shrimp are uniformly pink and coated with the plum sauce (about 4 minutes). Remove the shrimp to a serving dish and cover with the sauce from the pan. Combine this dish with curried rice and garnish with cilantro. Wonderful!

Serves 2

SHRIMP RÉMOULADE

Shrimp with rémoulade sauce makes a wonderful appetizer or light lunch. I prefer the flavor of shrimp boiled in spices but this dish can be made using shrimp cooked scampi style.

- **1 quart water**
- **1 bag crab boil spices (Pg.152)**
- **$^1/_2$ pound shelled and deveined medium shrimp**
- **1 cup rémoulade sauce at room temperature (Pg. 156)**
- **6 leaves of washed green leaf or bronze lettuce**

Add the crab boil spices to the water and bring to a boil. Drop in the shrimp and cook for 3 or 4 minutes until pink. Remove from the water and cool, then place in the refrigerator until chilled. Arrange the lettuce as a garnish on salad plates then arrange the shrimp on top in an attractive pattern. Spoon on the rémoulade sauce and serve.

2 servings

BROILED SHRIMP SATÉ

Saté sauce is a spicy Indonesian mixture which combines ground peanuts with soy sauce and curry. You can buy saté in Asian food markets or make your own.

- **12 peeled medium shrimp**
- **2 tablespoons Indonesian saté sauce (Pg. 157)**
  Parsley or cilantro for garnish

Marinate the shrimp in the saté sauce for 30 minutes in the refrigerator. Place the marinated shrimp in an oven-proof dish and place under the broiler for 5 minutes. Turn over once during the cooking. Remove the shrimp to a serving plate, cover with the cooking sauce and garnish with parsley or cilantro before serving.

Serves 2

SHRIMP SCAMPI #1

- **2 tablespoons butter**
- **2 tablespoons olive oil**
- **3 finely chopped green onions**
- **2 pressed cloves garlic**
- **2 tablespoons dry vermouth**
- **$1/2$ pound shelled and deveined fresh shrimp**
  Wedges of lemon or lime

Melt the butter and combine with the olive oil. Sauté the onion and garlic for about a minute. They will continue to cook when the shrimp are added. Add the vermouth and shrimp and heat to a simmer. Keep things moving in the pan. Turn the shrimp once for even cooking. 3 or 4 minutes should be enough. Shrimp are done when they have turned uniformly pink. Do not overcook as they will toughen. Remove to a serving dish. The shrimp can be eaten as is, or you can squeeze on a bit of lemon or lime juice.

As alternatives you can sauté some sliced mushrooms in the oil beforehand and you can shake a few dashes of Tabasco Sauce in the pan before adding the shrimp. Serve with garlic bread.

Serves 2

SHRIMP SCAMPI #2

This version makes a slightly heavier dish because of the addition of bread crumbs and Parmesan cheese. Nevertheless, it is wonderfully satisfying and a good alternative way of preparing delicious and different scampi.

- **2 tablespoons butter**
- **2 tablespoons olive oil**
- **3 dashes Tabasco Sauce**
- **2 pressed cloves garlic**
- **$1/2$ pound shelled and deveined shrimp**

$^1/_4$ **cup seasoned bread crumbs**
1   **tablespoon chopped capers**
       Freshly ground Parmesan cheese to taste

Melt the butter and combine with the olive oil. Sprinkle in the Tabasco and mix thoroughly. Lightly sauté the garlic, add the shrimp and continue to sauté until the shrimp are pink on both sides.

Remove the shrimp to a separate dish, leaving the juices in the pan. Stir in the seasoned bread crumbs and the capers and heat. Add the shrimp and stir to coat with the bread crumb mixture. The bread crumb mixture will not evenly coat the shrimp but will become part of the dish when served. Grate on the Parmesan while the pan is still hot. Serve hot or cold.

Serves 2

SHRIMP IN BEER BATTER

This deep fried dish is easy to make and creates a delicious dish of cooked shrimp encased in a thick beer batter.

10   **shelled large shrimp**
1   **quart Canola oil for deep frying**
THE BATTER
$^3/_4$ **cup flour**
1   **teaspoon baking powder**
1 $^1/_2$ **cups beer**
$^1/_2$ **teaspoon salt**
$^1/_4$ **teaspoon cayenne**
1   **egg yolk**
$^1/_2$ **teaspoon dill weed**
THE DIPPING SAUCE
$^1/_4$ **cup mayonnaise**
1 $^1/_2$ **teaspoons lemon juice**
$^1/_2$ **teaspoon dry dill weed**

To make the batter combine all the ingredients in a bowl and mix thoroughly. Let the batter sit for half an hour before using. Heat the oil to 375 degrees. Dip the shrimp in the batter, then place in the heated oil. Fry for 1 minute, turning once. Remove from the oil and drain on absorbent paper. Serve with the mayonnaise dipping sauce.

2 servings

BAKED POTATO STUFFED WITH AVOCADO AND SHRIMP

This is a wonderful way to surprise your guests with a baked potato concealing wonderful flavors. Easy to make and sure to win praise. Yes, the inside of the refilled potato does have a greenish cast. If this bothers you, serve it by candlelight.

- 2 (4 $\frac{1}{2}$ inch) baking potatoes, baked and allowed to cool
- $\frac{1}{4}$ cup ripe avocado
- 2 tablespoons finely chopped green onion - green part only
- 1 tablespoon finely chopped parsley
- 1 tablespoon Jalapeño Tabasco sauce
  Salt to taste
- 4 lightly sautéed and chopped medium shrimp

Cut an oval window into the top of each cooled baked potato and scoop out the pulp leaving $\frac{1}{4}$ inch clinging to the skin.

Mash the potato pulp with the avocado, onion, parsley and spices in a bowl until homogenous. Stir in the chopped shrimp. Stuff the potatoes with the mixture and replace the oval cap. Wrap in plastic wrap and set aside until needed. Place in the microwave for four or five minutes on medium setting until heated through and serve. You can also slice the cold stuffed potatoes and serve chilled as a snack.

Serves 2

SHRIMP POTATO SALAD

Here is a good way to vary the flavor of your potato salad using shrimp, sour cream and different herbs. This dish is both filling and delicious.

- 2 tablespoons butter
- 1 pressed clove garlic
- $\frac{1}{2}$ pound shelled, deveined and chopped shrimp
- 5 medium red potatoes cut into $\frac{3}{4}$ inch cubes
- $\frac{1}{2}$ cup sour cream
- $\frac{1}{2}$ cup pimientoed red pepper (Pg. 156)
- 2 teaspoons dried dill
- 1 teaspoon paprika
- $\frac{1}{2}$ cup chopped fresh parsley
  Salt and coarse ground pepper

Melt the butter in a sauce pan and sauté the garlic and the chopped shrimp until the shrimp is uniformly pink. Meanwhile, boil the potatoes until cooked but still firm. Drain and cool the potatoes, then mix in the shrimp, garlic and remaining ingredients. Chill before serving.

2 servings

SHRIMP IN WHITE WINE SAUCE

Here again we use the shrimp shells as part of the recipe to make a shrimp stock

1 $^1/_2$ **cups dry vermouth**
 $^1/_2$ **pound shelled and deveined medium shrimp (save the shells)**
 1 **bay leaf**
 $^1/_2$ **teaspoon thyme**
 $^1/_2$ **teaspoon rosemary**
 2 **tablespoons butter**
 $^1/_4$ **cup chopped white onion**
 2 **finely chopped cloves garlic**
 1 **tablespoon flour**
 1 **cup half-and-half**
 2 **tablespoons chopped parsley**
 Salt and pepper to taste

Put the wine in a sauce pan and bring to a boil. Add the shrimp and cook until the shrimp are uniformly pink turning as needed. Do not overcook. Remove the shrimp, set aside and coarsely chop when cool. Add the shrimp shells, bay leaf, thyme and rosemary to the wine and bring to a boil. Turn down the heat, cover and simmer for 15 minutes. Strain the liquid into a bowl and set aside. Discard the solids.

Melt the butter in a saucepan and sauté the onions and garlic over medium heat for 1 minute, then stir in the flour to make a paste. Add the half-and-half and blend the mixture allowing it to thicken slightly. Add the shrimp stock, the shrimp, parsley, salt and pepper and simmer for 5 minutes while stirring. Do not boil. Serve hot over white or brown rice with asparagus and a green salad. Note: This recipe can be changed dramatically by substituting cilantro for the parsley and adding a half tablespoon Jalapeño Tabasco sauce to the final mixture.

Serves 2

SHRIMP SAUCE WITH MANGO AND CURRY

If you like to explore the Asian markets as I do, you will notice that shrimp and mangoes are nearly staple items. I decided to combine these two delicacies to try making a shrimp/mango sauce to serve over rice. In making this sauce I used coconut milk instead of cream or half-and-half, and for spice I added curry powder. It is reminiscent of Thai cooking. Since that first cautious experiment I have enjoyed and served this interesting combination to many guests who have given it a high approval rate. Try it and see what you think.

> 3 tablespoons butter
> 8 large shelled and deveined shrimp (save the shells to make shrimp flavored rice)
> 2 pressed cloves of garlic
> 2 chopped green onions
> 1 tablespoon flour
> 1 cup coconut milk
> 1 teaspoon curry powder
> 1 cup chopped mango
> $^1/_2$ cup firm tofu cut into $^1/_2$ inch squares (optional)
> $^1/_2$ cup chopped cilantro
> 1 teaspoon salt

Melt the butter in a medium frying pan and sauté the shrimp on both sides until uniformly pink. Remove the shrimp from the pan and place on a cutting board. Add the garlic and chopped green onion to the pan and sauté for 1 minute over medium heat. Whisk the flour into the oil to make a paste and then add the cup of coconut milk and curry powder. Increase the heat and stir while the mixture thickens slightly. Chop the shrimp and add to the sauce with the mango, tofu, cilantro and salt. Heat while stirring and serve hot over shrimp flavored rice (see recipe Pg. 103)

Serves 2

SHRIMP CHOWDER

I love chowders and shrimp make some of the best. The shrimp flavor is unique and the red color of the shrimp and red potato skins make an attractive contrast with the green parsley and the white chowder.

> 2 strips bacon
> 3 cups water
> 3 medium red potatoes, cut into $^3/_4$ inch cubes with skin on
> $^1/_2$ cup chopped onion
> 2 finely chopped cloves garlic
> $^1/_2$ pound shelled and deveined shrimp each cut into four or five pieces
> 2 tablespoons olive oil
> 1 $^1/_2$ cups half-and-half
> $^1/_2$ cup chopped parsley
> $^1/_2$ teaspoon thyme

2   **tablespoons butter**
    Salt and pepper to taste
2   **teaspoons cream sherry**
    Oyster crackers

Cook the bacon until well done, drain and crumble. Set aside.

Bring the water to a boil, add the potatoes and cook for twenty minutes. Lightly sauté the onion, garlic and shrimp in olive oil for 1 $^1/_2$ minutes then add to the cooked potatoes and boiling water. Add the half- and-half, parsley, thyme, butter, salt and pepper and bring the mix to a simmer (do not boil). Serve immediately in soup bowls with a teaspoon of cream sherry poured on top. Oyster crackers add to the enjoyment.

Chowder for 2

SHRIMP TACO

This is what I call a "white taco" because the Ranch sauce is white and the cabbage is light in color. The taco can be varied by replacing the white sauce with any of the prepared "salsas" on the market. Some have more bite to them. Be careful not to stray too far from the milder sauce or the delicate shrimp flavor will be overwhelmed.

$^1/_2$ **cup Ranch dressing**
  1   **teaspoon Jalapeno Tabasco sauce (or other hot sauce)**
  4   **large shelled shrimp**
  1   **tablespoon canola oil**
  2   **pressed cloves garlic**
  2   **corn tortillas**
  2   **tablespoons chopped cilantro**
  2   **tablespoons chopped green onion - green part only**
$^1/_2$ **cup finely shredded cabbage**
$^1/_2$ **cup chopped tomato**
  1   **lemon wedge**

Make a sauce by mixing the ranch dressing with the Jalapeno Tabasco.

Prepare the shrimp by turning them over and making three or four cross cuts along the bottom to prevent them from curling when they are sautéed. Heat the oil and sauté both the shrimp and the garlic at the same time. Keep things moving so that the garlic does not burn and the shrimp cook evenly. Remove from the heat. In a separate pan heat the tortillas on both sides. Heap on a portion of the cilantro, green onion and shredded cabbage, cover with a dollop of the white sauce. Lay on two shrimp, a tablespoon of chopped tomato and place more of the sauce on top. Serve hot with a lemon wedge. For an interesting twist you can top with guacamole instead of the white sauce.

Makes 2 tacos.

SHRIMP MANICOTTI #1

     1   box manicotti shells (8)
    $\frac{1}{2}$ cup finely chopped onion
     4   finely chopped garlic cloves
     2   tablespoons olive oil
    $\frac{1}{2}$ cup pimientoed red bell pepper (Pg. 156)
    $\frac{1}{2}$ pound shelled and deveined large shrimp
    $\frac{1}{2}$ cup Italian style bread crumbs
    $\frac{1}{2}$ cup water
     2   tablespoons dry vermouth
    $\frac{1}{4}$ cup chopped pine nuts
    $\frac{1}{2}$ teaspoon thyme
     1   beaten egg
    $\frac{1}{2}$ cup freshly grated Parmesan cheese
    $\frac{1}{8}$ teaspoon cayenne pepper
         Salt and coarse ground pepper to taste
FOR THE SAUCE
     1   tablespoon butter
     1   tablespoon flour
    $\frac{1}{2}$ cup half-and-half
     1   tablespoon lemon juice
         Leftover stuffing mix

Heat the oven to 375 degrees.

Cook the manicotti according to instructions. Drain and temporarily set aside in cold water.

Sauté the onions and garlic in olive oil over medium heat for 1 minute, then add the red pepper. Chop the shrimp into $\frac{1}{4}$ inch pieces and mix with the onions, garlic and red pepper. Stir and cook until the shrimp pieces turn pink. In a bowl combine the bread crumbs, water, vermouth, pine nuts, thyme, egg, $\frac{1}{4}$ cup Parmesan cheese, cayenne, salt and black pepper. Add the sautéed vegetables and shrimp, and mix well. Stuff the Manicotti shells with the mixture and place in an oven-proof dish in a single layer.

To make the sauce, melt the butter in a pan and blend in the flour to make a paste. Mix in the half-and-half, lemon juice and any stuffing mix that remains. Heat while stirring to thicken slightly. Spread over the stuffed manicotti shells then sprinkle on the remaining Parmesan cheese. Cover with foil and bake for 45 minutes at 375 degrees.

Originally I said that this recipe "Serves 2, usually with leftovers." It doesn't. There are no leftovers. It is too good.

SHRIMP MANICOTTI #2

Here is an alternate manicotti recipe which includes spinach, Ricotta cheese and bacon to make a rich, tasty stuffing

- **1 box manicotti shells (8)**
- **3 finely chopped cloves garlic**
- **2 tablespoons butter**
- **$^1/_2$ pound shelled and deveined shrimp**
- **$^1/_2$ cup chopped mushrooms**
- **$^1/_2$ cup finely chopped green pepper**
- **1 tablespoon dried basil**
- **1 teaspoon coarse ground pepper**
- **1 cup Ricotta cheese**
- **$^1/_2$ cup chopped cooked spinach**
- **1 beaten egg**

FOR THE SAUCE
- **$^3/_4$ cup sour cream**
- **1 strip crisp cooked bacon - crumbled**
- **1 tablespoon freshly grated Mozzarella cheese**

Heat the oven to 375 degrees.

Cook the manicotti according to instructions. Drain and temporarily set aside in cold water.

Sauté the garlic in butter, add the shrimp and cook until uniformly pink. Remove the shrimp from the pan and set aside. In the same pan sauté the mushrooms and green pepper for about 5 minutes until soft, then the add the basil and pepper. Stir to prevent scorching. In a bowl combine the shrimp and vegetable mixture and add the ricotta cheese, spinach and beaten egg. Mix well. Stuff the manicotti and place in an oven-proof dish in a single layer. Spread the sour cream over the manicotti and then sprinkle with the crumbled bacon and grate on the Mozzarella cheese. Cover with aluminum foil and bake for 45 minutes in a 375 degree oven. Serve with white wine and crusty bread.

Serves 2

SHRIMP PASTA SAUCE

- 2 finely diced cloves garlic
- 2 chopped green onions
- $^1/_2$ medium tomato, chopped
- 3 tablespoons olive oil
- $^1/_2$ pound shelled and deveined medium shrimp sliced into $^1/_2$ inch pieces
- $^1/_2$ cup chopped cilantro
- $^1/_2$ cup half-and-half or sour cream
  Dash Jalapeño Tabasco or coarse ground pepper
  Dash of tarragon vinegar
- 8 ounces linguine or similar pasta, cooked as directed on package

Sauté the garlic, green onions and tomato in olive oil for 1 minute over medium heat. Add the shrimp pieces and stir until uniformly pink - do not overcook. Stir in the remaining ingredients and bring to a simmer. Serve over linguine with garlic bread and a green salad.

Sauce for 4 servings of pasta.

SHRIMP EGG ROLLS

These tasty Asian treats are also known as Spring Rolls because they are often served during the New Year Celebration of Spring Festival. Basically these are rolls which are made by filling flour dough wrappers with a mixture of vegetables and usually some kind of meat. In this recipe we use shrimp. Other seafood works as well. The filled rolls are then deep fried to a golden color. The flour wrappers can be purchased at many super-markets and Asian food stores.

- 1 pound shelled and deveined large shrimp
- 1 quart water
- 1 tablespoon sugar
- 1 teaspoon salt
- $^1/_2$ cup chopped cooked spinach
- $^1/_2$ cup chopped canned water chestnuts
- 4 cups finely chopped Napa cabbage
- 1 grated carrot
- 1 cup finely chopped celery
- 1 cup chopped soybean sprouts
- 3 chopped green onions
- 3 chopped cloves garlic
- 1 tablespoon cornstarch mixed with 1 tablespoon water
- 1 package 7" square egg roll wrappers
  Canola oil for deep frying

Boil the shrimp in the water for 3 minutes. Drain, cool and chop finely. Put the chopped shrimp in a bowl with the sugar, salt, spinach and water chestnuts. Mix the cabbage, carrots, celery, soybean sprouts, green onions and garlic and drop into boiling water for 10 to 15 seconds to wilt. The vegetables should remain crisp - do not overcook. Drain immediately and combine with the shrimp. Mix well and cool. This is your filling.

Combine the water and cornstarch to make a paste to seal the rolled wrappers.

To roll see the diagram below. 1: Lay out each egg roll wrapper at the diagonal and form 2 tablespoons of the filling in a 3 $^1/_2$ inch line just above the lower corner. 2: Place the lower corner of the wrapper over the filling and roll to the center. 3: Fold in the left and right ends. 4: Spread a bit of the water cornstarch mixture on the upper corner and fold back to form the roll. Lightly press in place to make the seal. Place the finished rolls on waxed paper or plastic wrap as they are made. The completed egg rolls can be cooked immediately, stored in the refrigerator for two or three days, or frozen for three months.

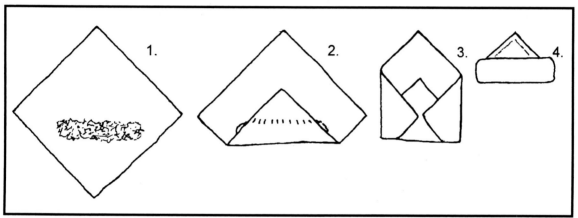

Folding the egg roll

To cook, heat the oil in a deep pan or deep fat fryer to a temperature of 375 degrees. Fry the rolls, two or three at a time, for 60 to 90 seconds or until golden brown. You may have to push the rolls down into the fat to insure that the wrapper browns evenly. Drain on absorbent paper. Reheat the oil to 375 degrees each time as you repeat the process with the other rolls. Serve hot with a dipping sauce (recipe follows.)

Makes about 16 egg rolls

DIPPING SAUCE
- 2 tablespoons oyster sauce (Soy sauce can be substituted)
- 1 tablespoon sherry
- 1 tablespoon rice vinegar (or white vinegar)
- 1 teaspoon sugar
- $^1/_4$ teaspoon freshly grated ginger (optional)

Mix ingredients and serve in individual small bowls for dipping.

Serves 2 for dipping

SHRIMP TEMPURA

My first introduction to Tempura Shrimp occurred in 1954 in a small Japanese village north of Mount Fuji. I was temporarily flying out of Atsugi Air Base, near Yokohama. I did not have a car, so for entertainment I used to go to the nearest local railway station and take any train heading west into the countryside. I would select a station at random, disembark and then prowl around the country roads and villages. In one of these small towns I came upon a tiny restaurant. There was a huge wok full of boiling oil near the front window, and the delicious smell of cooking shrimp was wafting out the front door. As always there was an outside display case featuring wax replicas of the food being offered. I wandered in, pointed to the wax model of tempura shrimp and embarked on a life long love of this delicacy.

In strict terms, the word "Tempura" refers to deep fried shrimp rather than to the cooking method, which is accurately described in Japanese as agamono, or frying in oil. Since most cultures have recipes that require deep frying the difference lies in the preparation and use of the batter. Japanese tempura batter should be prepared no more than ten minutes before use, and should be ice cold. The batter should coat the shrimp lightly, and when fried should have a crisp lacy texture.

> **Canola oil for frying**
> 10 **large shrimp - shelled and deveined**
> 1 **mixture of tempura batter (see below)**

Heat 3 inches of the oil to 375 degrees.

Prepare the shrimp ahead of time leaving the tail shell on. The shrimp can be split down the back if desired. Prepare the batter, making certain that it remains as cold as possible. Dip each shrimp in dry flour, then in the batter and drop into the 375 degree oil three at a time. Wear an apron and watch out for splatter. Let the shrimp cook for about a minute or until the batter is golden and crisp looking. Removed the shrimp from the oil and drain on absorbent paper. Be certain the oil is still at the required temperature, then repeat the process with the remaining shrimp. Serve the shrimp hot with a dipping sauce, if desired. Note that this type of cooking does not have to be restricted to shrimp. It lends itself well to other types of seafood - mussels, scallops, squid, fish fillets and the like, and certain vegetables like zucchini and crook necked squash, eggplant and mushrooms. Cook the vegetables for about a minute each.

TEMPURA BATTER

You can buy dry prepared Tempura batter in most Asiatic markets and the larger chain grocery stores, but it is simple to make if you wish to create your own.

> 1 **cup flour**
> $^1/_2$ **teaspoon baking powder**
> $^1/_2$ **teaspoon salt**
> 1 **lightly beaten egg yolk**
> 1 **cup ice water**

Sift the flour, baking powder and salt together. Combine the egg yolk and ice water and stir into the dry ingredients. Mix only until blended. Do not over mix. Place mixing bowl on a bed of ice to chill. Use within 10 minutes.

Makes about 2 cups of batter.

TENTSUYU SAUCE

This traditional tempura dipping sauce is available in canned or bottled form that is diluted for use.

- 1 cup chicken soup stock or water
- $1/3$ cup soy sauce
- $1/3$ cup Japanese mirin (or cream sherry)
- $1/4$ cup grated daikon radish (Asiatic markets)
- 2 tablespoons grated ginger root

Combine the first three ingredients and bring to a boil. Divide into serving cups. Add daikon and ginger and mix well.

Sauce for 4 people

SHRIMP TERIYAKI

- $3/4$ pound medium shrimp in their shells
- 3 tablespoons teriyaki sauce
- 2 tablespoons finely chopped sweet pickled ginger
- 2 pressed cloves garlic

Shell the shrimp and save the shells. Combine the teriyaki sauce, chopped ginger and pressed garlic, add the shrimp and mix well. Let the shrimp marinate in this mixture for at least an hour.

Place the shrimp on skewers lying on their side so that one "spoons" inside the next. Grill on a medium barbecue for 2 or 3 minutes to a side until the shrimp are pink and done. Spoon any extra marinade over the shrimp as they cook. Serve with chopped green onion sprinkled on top. Use the shells to make shrimp flavored rice (Pg. 103) to serve with this dish.

Serves 2

SWEET AND SOUR SHRIMP

  1   tablespoon canola oil
  2   chopped green onions
$^1/_3$ cup chopped green bell pepper
  2   finely chopped cloves of garlic
  6   snow peas
$^1/_4$ inch grated fresh ginger root
$^1/_2$ cup chopped bok choy cabbage
  1   cup sweet and sour sauce (Pg. 158)
12 peeled medium shrimp cut into two pieces

Heat the oil in a wok or frying pan until hot. Stir-fry all of the vegetables for one minute over high heat. Reduce the heat to medium and add the sweet and sour sauce and the shrimp. Continue to stir until the shrimp turn a uniform pink. Serve hot with rice.

Serves 2

MISCELLANEOUS SEAFOOD

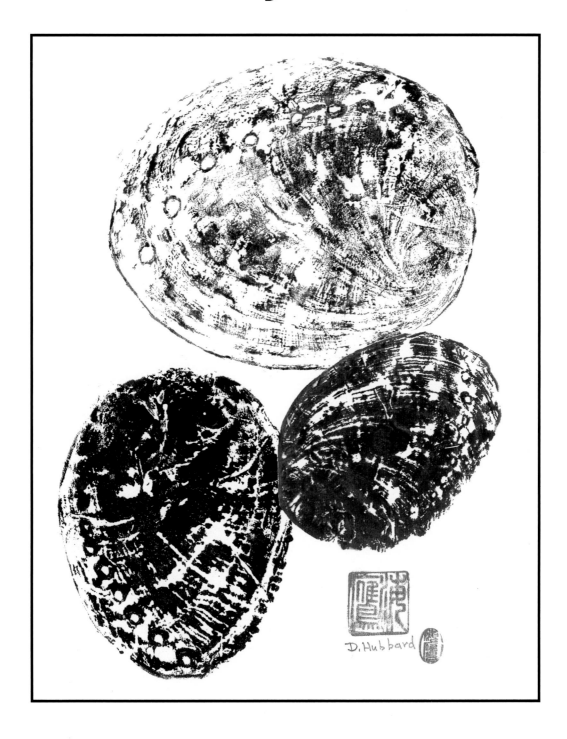

D. Hubbard

Overleaf:

California Abalone

MISCELLANEOUS SEAFOOD

RECIPES IN THIS SECTION

ABALONE

When I had my California scuba diving school (1969-72) you could find abalone under nearly every rock. Even beginning scuba divers could "limit out" of every dive. Now, because of the unrestricted use of scuba gear, abalone are a rarity in the southern part of the State, and even good divers have a hard time finding them. In northern California, however, abalone are still found in harvestable numbers due to the restriction on the use of "tanked air". Free divers who know what they are doing, and who are practiced in finding and removing these large mollusks from the rocks, can still bring in the allowed number.

CLEANING ABALONE

If you have the good fortune to find an abalone, bring it home and let it sit for at least an hour before cleaning. This allows the animal to relax and makes the process of removing the meat from its shell much easier. Once the abalone has relaxed pick it up so that it is inverted, and using a flat wooden or plastic tool like a rice paddle, quickly push down along the broad area of the shell against the base of the meaty foot. The connection between foot and shell is powerful and you must force the flat tool along so that the two parts separate. This may take more than one push, but eventually the meat/shell connection will be broken and the large foot and its connecting viscera can be removed.

Use a sharp knife and cut the entrails from the foot where they connect. Gently feel along the detached viscera to see if an abalone "pearl" has formed, and if so, remove and save. The pearls are not particularly valuable but they are attractive and can be used as decorations. Discard the entrails or plant them in the garden as fertilizer.

Rinse the meat and place the abalone foot on a cutting board. Carefully trim $^1/_8$ inch off the bottom to remove the "furry" sole with which the animal clings to the rock. This has an unpleasant texture and is very tough. Discard.

Trim the edges to remove the fringing black feelers and cut away the black covering membrane.

While still on the cutting board slice the remainder of the foot horizontally, across the grain, into $^3/_8$ inch steaks. Pound each steak with a meat mallet to tenderize. Do the tenderizing between two plastic bags. This will prevent splatter and keep the mallet and cutting board clean.

The meat is now ready to use in the recipes below.

ABALONE STEAKS

    2 prepared abalone steaks
    1 beaten egg
    1 cup seasoned bread crumbs
    4 tablespoons butter
       Salt
       Wedge of lemon

Dip the abalone in the egg and then in the bread crumbs to coat. Melt the butter in a frying pan and place each steak in the hot oil for about 20 seconds, then quickly turn over to cook the other side for 20 seconds. Do not overcook or the meat will toughen. Drain on absorbent paper, sprinkle with salt and serve with a lemon wedge. Excellent with rice, a green vegetable and chilled Mexican beer or white wine.

Serves 2

ABALONE RELLENOS

- 4 **prepared abalone steaks**
- 4 **teaspoons seeded and diced jalapeño chilies**
- 4 **tablespoons grated cheddar cheese**
  Sprinkle of garlic powder
- 8 **tablespoons butter**
- 2 **lemon wedges**

Bread the abalone steaks as directed in the previous recipe. Place a teaspoon of diced chilies along one edge of the flattened steak plus 1 tablespoon of grated cheese. Sprinkle with garlic powder and a touch of salt. Roll the abalone steak around the jalapeño/cheese mixture and pin the roll in place with toothpicks. To cook, melt 2 tablespoons of butter in a frying pan. Sauté the rolls one at a time for about 2 minutes turning them as you do so that all sides are cooked and the interior cheese melts. Drain on absorbent paper and serve hot with a lemon wedge. Add additional melted butter as needed for each roll.

Serves 2

ABALONE CHOWDER

- 3 **prepared abalone steaks chopped into small pieces**
- 1 **cup water**
- $^1/_2$ **cup chopped onion**
- 3 **finely chopped cloves of garlic**
- 1 **quart whole milk**
- $^1/_2$ **cup chopped cilantro**
- 2 **cooked and cubed medium red potatoes**
- 2 **slices crumbled crisp-cooked bacon**
- $^1/_2$ **teaspoon crushed dry thyme**
- $^1/_2$ **teaspoon worcestershire sauce**
  Salt and pepper to taste

Use a blender to grind the abalone pieces into smaller size. Put the cup of water in the blender before adding the meat to improve the grinder flow. In a sauce pan combine the abalone meat with the other ingredients. Simmer gently for ten minutes. Serve with toasted garlic bread and green salad.

You can use Top Snail or conch meat in place of abalone in this recipe.

Serves 2

CRAWFISH

(Crayfish, crawdads) are small fresh water crustaceans found in vast numbers in the wetlands of Louisiana, Mississippi and East Texas. They are also found in lesser numbers in many other parts of the country.

I know that they are found in New York State. The first (and only) time I played hooky from P.S. 46, my grammar school in the Bronx, my pal, Rodney, and I were lured away by another friend who told of finding small "lobsters" in the Bronx River where it ran through the Bronx Botanical Gardens. This particular day was a Jewish holiday. We knew that most of the Jewish kids would not be going to school so we decided that our absence would not be noticed. The three of us took off for the river. Sure enough, we found at least a half dozen of these small crustaceans hiding around and under the rocks in the river. There were probably many more, but both Rod and I were "gun shy" of anything with claws. We had cut our crabbing teeth on the fast moving, hard biting blue-clawed crabs in Long Island Sound. As for playing hooky, both Jeff and I were missed and turned in by our teachers, and we caught it from our folks. That was the last time I played hooky until High School when I could not resist the lure of a beautiful Spring day and the nearby Bronx Zoo. This time I did not get caught.

As for crawfish, they do look like small lobsters, both in coloration and shape. They average about an ounce each. In the South, where there are uncountable numbers of them, they are cooked in vats and served in mounds. The hungry diners tear into them, twisting and pulling the meat from the tail and sucking the juices out of the head. These small crustaceans also make a great ingredient for sea food stews and for appetizers.

In some of the more diverse sea food markets you can buy cooked crawfish tail meat already extracted from the shell. In California these small shrimp-sized meats are labeled "langostinos", Spanish for small or baby lobster. The meat has a very delicate crab flavor and can be used in any recipes calling for crab or lobster.

CRAWFISH COURT BOUILLON

This is one of many popular mixtures for cooking crawfish and adding flavor to the meat. Many prepared pre-packaged mixtures are also available if you wish to save time.

- 1 **chopped stalk celery**
- 1 **bay leaf**
- $^1/_2$ **cup chopped onion**
- 2 **finely chopped garlic cloves**
- $^1/_4$ **cup chopped parsley or cilantro**
- 2 **dashes Tabasco**
- 2 **quarts water**
- $^1/_4$ **teaspoon cayenne pepper**
- 50 **live crawfish**

Set the crawfish aside and bring all of the ingredients to a rapid boil. Simmer for ten minutes to blend the flavors. Return to a rapid boil and plunge the crawfish into the liquid. Cook for about 10 minutes until they have all turned bright red. Drain and serve with garlic bread and good ice cold beer.

Serves 2 to 4

LANGOSTINO SALAD

$^1/_2$ pound cooked crawfish tails removed from shells
2 finely sliced stalks celery
3 finely sliced green onions
$^1/_2$ cup chopped tomato
$^1/_2$ cup mayonnaise
$^1/_2$ teaspoon dry dill weed
1 teaspoon sugar or one packet NutraSweet (Equal)
Salt and pepper to taste

Combine all the ingredients and mix well. Serve cold on toast points or lettuce leaves.

Salad for 2

LIMPETS

Back in the early 1970s when I was running scuba diving tours in Baja, Mexico, I often invited one of my children and a friend to come along just for fun. To keep them busy I would have them gather limpets from the rocks around the tide line. These I would later clean and make into a "limpet stew" for the kids. Appreciate that these youngsters had probably never eaten any seafood more exciting than a boneless filet with a cream sauce. But peer pressure and a hearty outdoor appetite always won out. The saying: "Hunger makes the best sauce!" is appropriate here. Lauren, my youngest daughter insisted that the recipe be included in this book. She was right, of course!

In California and the ocean side of Baja there are large "Owl Limpets". This limpet takes its name from the markings on the inside of the shell which resemble a horned owl. They *are* large and can reach 4 inches in length, although most measure 2 $^1/_2$ inches or less. Limpets are found at the tide line, with some below and some above. You harvest them using a small knife which you slide under the shell and then use as a pry. In a sense limpets are like small abalone and must be cleaned in much the same way. After gathering the limpets invert the shell and use a small sharp knife to cut between the animal and the shell until it is released. Turn the meat over and cut away the viscera. Rinse the cleaned meat in sea water before using.

LIMPET STEW

     1   cup fresh limpet meats chopped into $^1/_4$ inch pieces
     1   cup rice
     2   cups water
     1   (8 ounce) can tomato sauce
     1   teaspoon sugar
     3   chopped garlic cloves
     1   teaspoon thyme
     3   tablespoons butter or (for camping trips) margarine

Place all ingredients in a cooking pot and bring to a boil. Simmer for 14 minutes until the rice is cooked. Serve to hungry campers with Mexican bolillos or chunks of Italian bread.

Serves 2 hungry kids and a dad

SEA SNAILS

All snails are edible and have a distinct marine flavor. Many, like the Top Snails in the Pacific, contain a lot of meat. The meat comes from the animal's "foot", and because it is thickened muscle it is generally tough. With the smaller snails this does not matter much. With larger species it is best to pound them with a mallet to tenderize them or even slice them into thin wafers before eating. I prepare all snails by boiling them in the shell. Cook small snails for 10 minutes, and the larger Top Snails for 15. Save the cooking water. It makes a nice sea food broth.

The meat is extracted from cooked snails by piercing with a small fork and then twisting in the direction of the spiral. The meat will usually come out with the entrails and operculum (the hard calcareous covering at the front) still attached. Cut off the entrails and the operculum and rinse the meat. Pound and slice the larger pieces to tenderize. You can eat the meat as is, but it is better if it is dipped into melted butter or one of the many tasty sauces. The meat can also be used in salads (see below), chowders and other sea food applications.

JAPANESE SPICED SNAILS

Preparing small snails takes a few extra minutes, but they are noticeably more tender than their larger brethren, and you can usually gather them quickly from the inter-tidal zone. All of them are edible.

     1   tablespoon soy sauce
     2   tablespoons Japanese mirin wine (or cream sherry)
     1   teaspoon sugar
    50   cooked periwinkles

Combine the soy sauce, mirin wine and sugar and mix well. Remove the meat from the snails as directed above and marinate the snail meat in the mixture overnight. Serve with toothpicks as an appetizer. Fifty $^1/_2$ inch diameter periwinkles will give you about $^1/_4$ cup of meat.

SEA SNAIL PASTA SALAD

- 1/2 package (8 ounces) small shell pasta
- 2 tablespoons olive oil
- 1/4 cup pimientoed red pepper (Pg. 1586
- 1 teaspoon dried dill
- 1 thinly sliced stalk celery
  Juice from one lime
- 2 tablespoons thinly sliced leek or green onion
- 1/2 cup finely chopped Top Snail meat
  Salt and freshly ground black pepper
- 1/2 cup Ranch Dressing

Cook the pasta as instructed on the package, drain and mix with 2 tablespoons of olive oil. Add all the remaining ingredients and place in the refrigerator to chill before serving.

Serves 2

SPINY SEA URCHIN

The roe of the spiny sea urchin has been considered a delicacy in Japan and the Mediterranean for centuries but due to over-harvesting the supply in the waters adjacent to those areas is limited. Conversely there are large numbers available in the waters off the American West Coast and New England. These are harvested in limited numbers and the roe is extracted and flown to overseas destinations. Very little urchin is eaten in the United States and that mostly by new arrivals from overseas. This is unfortunate because the roe is tasty, abundant and easily prepared.

The urchin is related to the starfish. This becomes evident when you extract the roe which is set up in five separate fingers within the shell (test). The yellow or pinkish roe has a sweet, slightly briny flavor which is excellent eaten as is or with a squeeze of lemon or lime juice. It can also be used on crackers or toast as an hors d'oeuvre. It is not "fishy". The flavor (not the texture) is more akin to raw clam than any other taste with which to compare.

In Japanese it is called UNI and is eaten as sushi on top of seaweed wrapped rice.

CLEANING SEA URCHIN

To remove the roe you invert the urchin and break out a 1 1/2 inch circular area around the center. Do this with the point of a knife or cut with strong scissors. Rinse out the messy stuff, mostly dark membranes and small particles of chewed kelp, then use an inverted spoon to "peel" the roe from the inside surface.

SEA URCHIN ROE SPAGHETTI SAUCE

2 cloves finely chopped garlic
2 chopped green onions
2 tablespoons butter
$1/4$ teaspoon thyme
$1/4$ avocado, cut into small squares
4 seeded and halved medium black olives
1 tablespoon chopped parsley
   Chopped roe from 2 large urchins

Sauté the garlic and onion in the butter with the thyme. Add the avocado, olives, parsley and urchin roe. Cook about 2 minutes over low heat while stirring, just long enough to heat the ingredients through. Serve over hot pasta.

Makes sauce for 2 servings

URCHIN ROE APPETIZER

   Roe from 2 large urchins (10 pieces)
2 tablespoons grated red onion
1 tablespoon olive oil
$1/4$ cup chopped parsley
   Small sprig chopped fresh basil
   Sprinkle of garlic powder
2 slices of toasted bread cut into quarters
   Salt and pepper to taste

Combine the first six ingredients and chill in the refrigerator. Serve with toast points and salt and pepper as an appetizer.

Makes appetizers for 2

SEA URCHIN ROE SPREAD

   Finely chopped roe from 2 large urchins
3 tablespoons reduced fat mayonnaise
1 tablespoon grated red onion
$1/2$ cup sour cream
1 tablespoon lemon juice
   Sprinkle of garlic powder
   Salt and pepper to taste

Mix ingredients and let stand in the refrigerator overnight. Serve as a dipping sauce with bread sticks or use as a spread.

SEA URCHIN ROE SPREAD (GREEK)

    8 slices white bread with crusts removed
    2 tablespoons water
       Roe from 2 large urchins
$^3/_4$ cup olive oil
    4 tablespoons lemon juice
    1 teaspoon grated onion

Moisten the bread with water and squeeze to remove the excess. Combine with the urchin roe in a small bowl and mash and knead together to form a paste. Blend in the olive oil, then the lemon and finally knead in the grated onion. Serve the spread on saltine crackers or bagels. Refrigerate any excess for later use.

Makes about one cup of spread

SEA URCHIN ROE IN BUTTER AND CREAM

    1 tablespoon butter
    1 tablespoon half-and-half
       Roughly chopped roe from 2 large urchins

Melt butter in a small sauce pan, stir in cream to blend. Add the urchin roe and gently heat. Serve on rice or on San Francisco sour dough bread.

Serves 1

SEA URCHIN ROE WITH MARINATED ARTICHOKE HEARTS

       Roe from 2 large urchins
    2 chopped marinated artichoke hearts
    1 tablespoon lemon juice
       Freshly ground pepper

Place the roe pieces on a small dish and slice into $^1/_2$ inch segments. Mix with the chopped artichoke hearts and lemon juice. Grate on the pepper and serve on toast.

Serves 1

SEA URCHIN ROE OMELET

$^1/_4$ cup finely chopped seeded green bell pepper
$^1/_4$ cup chopped tomato
  1 tablespoon grated red onion
  1 finely diced clove garlic
  2 tablespoons olive oil
$^1/_4$ cup milk
  2 lightly beaten eggs
     Mashed roe from two sea urchins

Sauté the green pepper, tomato, onion and garlic in olive oil until tender. Set aside. Mix the eggs and milk and pour into an oiled, heated pan. As the mixture begin to congeal, tilt the pan and pull the hardening egg mixture towards the upper edge, allowing the still liquid part of the egg to run on to the empty pan. When the omelet is nearly formed distribute the urchin roe evenly along the center and cover with the cooked vegetables. Fold first one side of the omelet and then the other across the center mixture. Sprinkle with salt and pepper and serve with toast.

Makes an omelet for 1

COMBINATION DISHES

D. Hubbard

Overleaf:
*Sally Lightfoot Crab
and Friends*

COMBINATION DISHES

BOUILLABAISSE

This is one of those wonderful seafood combinations that can rightfully be called a Mediterranean Fish chowder. It should be prepared in a large Dutch oven or casserole and served immediately after the last shellfish is cooked. Just the smell of it cooking is worth the price.

- 1 small chopped onion
- 2 finely chopped cloves garlic
- $^1/_3$ cup olive oil
- 1 (14.5 ounce) can whole peeled tomatoes with juice
- 1 teaspoon sugar
- 1 teaspoon dried thyme
   Pinch of fennel
   Pinch of saffron
- 1 bay leaf
   Salt and coarse ground pepper to taste
- $^1/_3$ cup chopped fresh parsley
- 3 $^1/_2$ cups water
- $^1/_2$ cup dry vermouth
- 1 pound firm white fish cut into pieces
- $^1/_2$ pound bay scallops
- $^1/_2$ cup chopped, cooked octopus pieces
- $^1/_2$ cup blanched and sliced calamari (squid)
   Other shellfish:crabs/lobster/shrimp (optional)
- 8 mussels in shell
- 8 small hard clams in shell

In a 4 quart Dutch oven sauté the onion and garlic in olive oil. Add tomatoes (broken up) with their juice, sugar and spices (thyme/fennel/saffron/bay leaf/salt/pepper). Bring to a boil, reduce heat and simmer for half an hour to blend flavors. Add the parsley, water, vermouth and seafood (less the mussels and clams). Simmer ten minutes. Add the mussels and clams and simmer until they open, about 5 minutes. Serve in deep soup bowls with crusty bread and a good red wine.

Serves 4

CIOPPINO

This is one of the regional, allegedly California, dishes that uses whatever seafood is available in varying quantities.

- $^1/_4$ cup olive oil
- 2 minced cloves garlic
- 2 cups chopped red onions
- 1 seeded and chopped green pepper
- 1 (14.5 ounce) can peeled and broken up tomatoes (or 2 fresh - chopped)
- 1 (8 ounce) can tomato sauce
- 2 cups dry red wine
- 2 teaspoons dried oregano
- $^1/_2$ teaspoon dried basil
- 1 bay leaf
  Salt and pepper to taste
- $^1/_2$ pound blanched and sliced calamari (squid) and tentacles
- $^1/_2$ pound firm white fish sliced into chunks
- $^1/_2$ pound cooked and chopped octopus (optional)
- $^1/_2$ pound crab or lobster chunks (optional)
- $^1/_2$ pound shelled raw shrimp
- $^1/_2$ pound scallops
- 8 mussels in shell
- 8 small hard clams in shell
- $^1/_3$ cup cilantro for garnish when served.

Heat the olive oil and sauté garlic, onions and green peppers for 1 or 2 minutes until the onions are opaque and the green peppers soften. Add tomatoes, tomato sauce, wine, spices and squid. Simmer 20 minutes - stir often. Add fish and other seafood less mussels and clams - simmer 6 minutes more. Add the mussels and clams in shells. Cook for an additional 5 minutes until shell fish are open. Serve in large bowls with cilantro garnish on top. Goes well with toasted sourdough bread, Caesar salad and red wine.

Serves 4

JAMBALAYA

  1 chopped large onion
  2 finely chopped cloves garlic
  1 cup diced green bell pepper
  2 tablespoons olive oil
  1 (14.5 ounce) can peeled and broken up tomatoes
$^1/_2$ teaspoon dried thyme
$^1/_2$ teaspoon dried oregano
$^1/_4$ teaspoon cayenne pepper
  1 bay leaf
$^1/_4$ cup chopped cilantro
  4 strips crisp cooked bacon
  1 cup bottled clam juice or chicken broth
  2 cups cooked rice
  1 pound cubed chicken meat
  1 pound cleaned and sliced squid plus tentacles
  1 pound shelled shrimp
     Salt as desired

Sauté onions, garlic and green pepper in olive oil until green pepper is limp. About 2 minutes. Add tomatoes and spices. Bring to simmer and add cilantro. Chop up bacon and add with the clam juice (or chicken broth). Stir in the cooked rice, chicken, and squid. Simmer for 20 minutes. Add the raw shrimp and cook for an additional 5 minutes until the shrimp turn pink. Serve in soup bowls with French rolls and green salad. Since this is a true ethnic Creole dish ingredients can vary depending on what is on hand.

Serves 4

LOUISIANA SEAFOOD GUMBO

As with so many seafood stews, gumbo can be made in an infinite number of ways. The final result will depend on what ingredients are available and the whims of the cook. Gumbo is a combination dish which derives its character from the mixed indian, negro, French, Spanish and Acadian background of the Louisiana people. Gumbo is a grayish/brownish color, but if tomatoes are added, as they sometimes are, it can tint toward the red. Cooks choice. Most importantly, the flavor of gumbo is unique and different (hot) from the majority of seafood stews with a European origin.

1	coarsely chopped large onion
3	finely chopped cloves garlic
$^1/_4$	cup canola oil
2	seeded and chopped jalapeño peppers
1	chopped medium green bell pepper
2	bay leaves
$^1/_2$	teaspoon cayenne pepper
$^1/_4$	teaspoon thyme
3	cups water
1	cup dry red wine
3	splashes Tabasco sauce
6	cooked crawfish
8	freshly shucked oysters with juices
2	cooked crabs - cleaned and split
8	shelled medium shrimp
$^1/_4$	pound coarsely chopped ham
4	skinned chicken thighs
1	tablespoon brown roux (Pg.154)
$^1/_2$	teaspoon filé powder
2	cups cooked white rice
1	bunch fresh cilantro

In a 2 gallon Dutch oven sauté the onion and garlic in the canola oil for about a minute. Add the jalapeño and green peppers, bay leaves, cayenne pepper, thyme, water, wine and Tabasco. Bring to boil and then simmer for 30 minutes. Add the seafood, ham and chicken and cook for an additional 25 minutes to blend flavors. Mix in the brown roux and filé powder. Stir well until the gumbo is thickened slightly. Do not return to a boil (filé, which is used as a thickener, becomes stringy when boiled). Serve in wide soup bowls with $^1/_2$ cup white rice in the center of each. Garnish with cilantro. Chilled beer is the accompaniment.

Serves 4

PAELLA

Paella takes its name from the Spanish vessel in which it is prepared (paellera).

$^1/_3$ cup olive oil
  8 skinned chicken thighs or 4 halved skinless and boneless chicken breasts.
  1 chopped chorizo (or sweet Italian sausage)
  2 finely chopped cloves garlic
  2 chopped medium onions
  1 seeded and chopped red bell pepper
$^1/_2$ teaspoon saffron
  1 (14.5 ounce) can peeled tomatoes
  6 marinated artichoke hearts
$1^1/_2$ cups uncooked white rice
  3 cups water
  1 teaspoon salt
$^1/_4$ cup chopped ham
  1 pound shelled shrimp with tail shell on
  8 mussels in the shell
  8 small hard shelled clams
  6 pre-cooked crawfish
  3 tablespoons chopped parsley
  1 cup fresh or frozen peas

Preheat oven to 425 degrees.

Heat the olive oil in a frying pan and fry the chicken pieces until golden. Remove the chicken and set aside. Add the chorizo, garlic, onion, red bell pepper and saffron. Cook for 2 minutes. Mix in the tomato and artichoke hearts and bring to a simmer. Place the rice in the center of a paella dish (or 4 quart oven-proof casserole) with 3 cups of water and the salt. Pour on the contents of the frying pan, the chicken pieces and ham. Cover with foil and put in oven for 20 minutes. Add shellfish (except the crawfish) and cook 10 minutes longer until the rice is done. Remove from the oven and stir the mixture to distribute the cooked items. Remove all the cooked clam meats from the shell and half the mussel meats and mix into the dish. Sprinkle on the peas and parsley and arrange the cooked crayfish and remaining meat-filled mussel shells artfully on top. Cover with the foil again and let the dish sit for 10 minutes before serving to heat the peas and crawfish. Serve with a green salad with an oil and vinegar dressing and chilled white table wine for an authentic Spanish dish.

Serves 4

CLAMS AND CALAMARI/OCTOPUS PASTA TOPPING

This is an easy way to vary the topping placed on pasta dishes. Obviously the seafoods can be changed to suit availability and your own taste.

$^1/_2$ pound linguine
2 tablespoons olive oil (divided use)
1 (6.5 ounce) can chopped clams - reserve the juice
$^1/_2$ cup cooked chopped octopus   (or)
$^1/_2$ cup blanched and sliced calamari (squid)
1 tablespoon butter
$^1/_4$ teaspoon garlic powder
$^1/_4$ teaspoon thyme
   Freshly ground Parmesan cheese.

Cook the linguine as specified on package. Toss with 1 tablespoon of the olive oil. Set aside and keep warm. Combine the remaining ingredients and half the clam juice in a frying pan and heat on the stove until well warmed. Pour the mix over linguine top with grated Parmesan and serve. Garlic bread and a good chilled dry white wine are a suggested compliment.

Pasta topping for 2

CRAB MEAT AND CLAM PASTA

$^1/_2$ pound linguine
3 tablespoons olive oil (divided use)
$^1/_2$ cup chopped onion
2 finely chopped cloves garlic
4 sliced medium mushrooms
1 tablespoon cream sherry
$^1/_2$ pound shredded crab meat or shredded imitation crab (surimi)
1 can of chopped clams, drained
$^2/_3$ cup half-and-half
   Salt and pepper to taste
$^1/_2$ cup chopped parsley
$^1/_4$ teaspoon paprika

Cook the pasta as directed on the package, drain and coat with 1 tablespoon olive oil. Sauté onions, garlic and mushrooms in the remaining oil until the mushrooms are limp. Mix in the sherry. Add the crab, clams and half-and-half. Bring to a simmer. In large bowl combine the pasta with the sauce. Sprinkle on the paprika. Garnish with parsley and serve with a sliced tomato salad and chilled dry white wine.

Serves 2

SEAFOOD CASSEROLE

  8 ounces medium elbow macaroni
  1 tablespoon olive oil
10 small hard clams
  1 tablespoon dry vermouth
  2 tablespoons water
  3 tablespoons butter (divided use)
  3 finely chopped cloves garlic
10 shelled medium shrimp
$1/2$ pound bay scallops or quartered sea scallops
  5 sliced medium mushrooms
  2 teaspoons fresh rosemary leaves
$1/4$ cup chopped parsley
  1 tablespoon lemon juice
  4 ounces shredded mozzarella cheese
$1/2$ medium avocado, cut into $1/2$ inch chunks
$1/2$ cup half-and-half
     Salt and coarsely ground pepper to taste
  1 cup bread crumbs
  1 additional tablespoon butter, diced

Heat the oven to 350 degrees

Cook the macaroni as directed on the package, drain and mix in 1 tablespoon olive oil to coat. Set aside in a mixing bowl.

Steam the clams in the vermouth and water until the clams are open. Set aside to cool. Melt 2 tablespoons butter in a frying pan and sauté the garlic with the shrimp and scallops until the shrimp is uniformly pink. When cool remove the clams from their shells and add to the sautéed seafood along with any pan juices. Add the mushrooms, rosemary, parsley and the combined seafoods to the macaroni. Pour on the lemon juice, add the mozzarella cheese, avocado chunks, half-and-half, salt and pepper and mix well until all the ingredients are distributed. Pour into an oiled casserole dish, sprinkle on the bread crumbs, dot with butter and bake at 350 degrees for 30 minutes until the bread crumbs are brown. Remove from oven and let sit for 20 minutes before serving. Garlic bread, a green salad with ranch dressing and a dry white wine round out the meal.

Serves 6

SHRIMP AND SCALLOP FETTUCINE

$^1/_4$ pound (1 stick) butter
  5 finely chopped cloves garlic
$^1/_2$ pint half-and-half
$^1/_4$ pound peeled medium shrimp chopped into $^1/_2$ inch pieces
$^1/_4$ pound bay or quartered sea scallops
  1 package (16 ounces) fettuccine or flat egg noodles
     Freshly grated Parmesan cheese
     Salt and pepper to taste
  1 teaspoon nutmeg

Bring sufficient water to boil to cook noodles when needed.

To make the seafood sauce: melt the butter and sauté the garlic for 1 minute over medium heat. Add the half-and-half. Heat and stir continuously in frying pan until large bubbles form. Add the shrimp and scallops and continue stirring until shrimp has turned pink. Remove from stove and keep warm.

Cook the pasta as directed on the package, drain and place in a large bowl. Pour on the sauce and sprinkle with Parmesan cheese, salt, pepper and nutmeg. Toss to mix and serve with a cold, crisp salad (Caesar dressing is good choice) and a dry white wine.

Serves 2

SHRIMP AND SCALLOP PASTA SALAD

  8 ounces ($^1/_2$ package) small sea shell pasta
  2 tablespoons olive oil (divided use)
  1 tablespoon butter
  4 finely chopped garlic cloves
$^1/_3$ pound shelled and chopped small shrimp
$^1/_3$ pound halved bay scallops
$^1/_2$ cup pimientoed sweet red pepper (Pg. 156)
$^1/_2$ cup chopped radish sprouts
  1 tablespoon lemon juice
  1 teaspoon dried basil flakes
  1 teaspoon Jalapeño Tabasco sauce
$^1/_2$ cup buttermilk/sour cream sauce (Pg. 151) or substitute $^1/_2$ cup Ranch Dressing

Cook the pasta as directed on the package, rinse and toss with one tablespoon of the olive oil. Set aside to cool. In a small sauce pan melt the butter and combine with the remaining olive oil. Sauté the garlic in the oil for one minute and then add the shrimp and scallops. Continue cooking over medium heat until the shrimp pieces are uniformly pink. Combine all ingredients and chill in the refrigerator before serving.

Salad for 4

141

SEAFOOD LASAGNA (LASAGNA FRUTTI DI MARE)

  6   strips lasagna noodles
$^1/_2$ cup water
  2   tablespoons dry vermouth
  6   small hard clams in shell
  4   mussels in shell
$^1/_4$ cup olive oil (divided use)
  3   finely chopped cloves garlic
10 shelled medium shrimp
  4   blanched and sliced calamari
$^1/_4$ cup cooked octopus
$^1/_2$ cup chopped onion
  4   chopped large mushrooms
$^1/_4$ chopped green bell pepper
$^1/_2$ cup chopped fresh parsley
  1   teaspoon dried oregano
     Salt and pepper to taste
$^1/_2$ cup ricotta cheese
$^1/_2$ cup grated mozzarella cheese
     White sauce as outlined below
     Parmesan cheese for grating

Heat oven to 375 degrees

Cook the lasagna noodles for half the time given in the instructions, drain and place in cold water until ready to use.

Combine the water and vermouth, add the clams and mussels, bring to a boil and steam the shell fish until open (about 3-5 minutes). Cool slightly and remove the meat from the shells. If the mussels are too large cut in half.

Pour half the olive oil in a sauce pan, add the garlic and shrimp and sauté until the shrimp have turned pink on both sides. Mix in the clam and mussel meats and their juices and the octopus and squid. Stir once or twice to coat all the pieces and then transfer to a bowl for later use.

Put the remaining olive oil in the sauce pan and sauté the onions, mushrooms, green pepper and parsley until cooked and limp. Sprinkle with oregano, salt and pepper to taste. Mix well.

In a square 9 inch oven-proof dish place a layer of lasagna noodles, cover with half the seafood mixture and juices, spoon on half the sautéed vegetables and then dot with ricotta cheese and grated mozzarella. Place a second layer of pasta on top and then repeat the layering with the remaining seafood and vegetables plus ricotta and mozzarella. Top with the final pieces of pasta and then spread on the white sauce and grate on a heavy layer of Parmesan.

Bake covered at 375 degrees for 35 minutes until cheese on top is melted and slightly browned. Let sit for 10 minutes before serving. Serve with garlic bread and a green salad.

WHITE SAUCE FOR LASAGNA

- 2 **tablespoons butter**
- 1 **tablespoon flour**
- $^1/_2$ **cup half-and-half**
- 1 **tablespoon sherry**

Melt the butter in a non-stick sauce pan, whisk in the flour then add the half-and-half and sherry. Stir over medium heat until the mixture thickens slightly.

Serves 4

SEAFOOD QUICHE

- 2 **tablespoons butter**
- 3 **finely chopped cloves garlic**
- 1 **finely chopped medium onion**
- $^1/_4$ **cup bay scallops**
- $^1/_4$ **cup medium shrimp, chopped into $^1/_4$ inch pieces.**
- 6 **beaten eggs**
- $^1/_2$ **cup half-and-half**
- 2 $^1/_2$ **cups grated Swiss cheese ($^1/_2$ pound grated solid Swiss)**
- $^1/_2$ **cup cooked, chopped and drained spinach**
- 1 **teaspoon thyme**
- 1 **teaspoon basil**
- 1 **teaspoon pepper**
- $^1/_2$ **teaspoon salt**
  Shake of garlic powder
  One single dish pie dough recipe
  Sprinkle of nutmeg for topping

Heat oven to 350 degrees

Melt the butter in a pan and lightly sauté garlic, onion, scallops and shrimp until shrimp turns pink. Let cool. Combine the eggs, half- and-half, cheese and spinach. Add the seasonings and the sautéed garlic, onion and seafood. Line a 10" quiche pan or oiled pie plate with dough and pour in the seafood custard mix. Add a sprinkle of nutmeg and bake at 350 degrees for 45 minutes or until mixture is cooked through and set. Depending on what is available you can add or substitute cooked crab, diced octopus, squid, clams, mussel meats, etc.

Serves 2

SHRIMP AND CHICKEN WITH SOUR CREAM/DILL SAUCE

- 1 recipe for sour cream/dill sauce (Pg. 157)
- 2 boneless, skinless chicken breasts
- 2 tablespoons butter
- 2 finely chopped cloves garlic
- 2 thinly sliced green onions
- 6 peeled and butterflyed large shrimp
- 1 tablespoon capers for garnish
- 2 sprigs parsley for garnish
  Salt and pepper to taste

Prepare the sour cream/dill sauce, set aside and keep warm.

Lay chicken breasts on cutting board and gently pound with a meat mallet to tenderize and flatten. Melt the butter in a pan and lightly sauté the garlic and onions. Add the chicken breasts and sauté on both sides until slightly browned and cooked through. Set aside. Add the shrimp and cook until evenly pink on both sides. Place each chicken breast on a plate with four shrimp attractively arranged on and around the meat. Cover with 2 tablespoons of the prepared sauce plus 8 - 10 capers and a sprig of parsley. Serve with brown rice and string beans. Goes well with a salt-rimmed margarita.

Serves 2

STUFFED GREEN PEPPERS WITH SHRIMP AND CRAB

- 4 green bell peppers
- 2 cups cooked rice
- 3 chopped green onions
- 12 cooked, shelled and roughly chopped shrimp
- $1/4$ cup cooked crab meat or shredded imitation crab (surimi)
- $1/4$ teaspoon garlic powder
- $1/4$ teaspoon coarse ground pepper
  Salt to taste
- 2 tablespoons caper sauce (Pg. 151)

Heat oven to 350 degrees

Remove the tops from the green peppers and empty the contents of seeds and veins. Parboil for 8 minutes, drain and cool. Combine the rice, shrimp, crab, green onions, garlic powder, pepper and salt. Fill each of the pepper cases with the mixture and place in an oven-proof baking dish. Cover with foil and bake in the oven for 15 minutes until heated through. Top with caper sauce and serve with boiled potatoes and a green salad.

Serves 2

SEAFOOD CALZONE AND PIZZA

We all know what pizza is, but less is known about calzone which is pizza dough filled with assorted ingredients and then folded over to form an Italian turnover. A small seafood pizza or calzone can be made ahead and reheated in the microwave or served as a satisfying cold lunch.

PIZZA DOUGH

    1   **packet active dry yeast**
1 $^1/_2$ **teaspoons sugar**
    1   **cup hot water (95 - 105 degrees F.)**
    3   **cups all-purpose flour**
    1   **teaspoon salt**
  $^1/_3$ **cup olive oil**

Add the water to an oven-proof cup or small bowl and heat to proper temperature. Dissolve the sugar in the water, then add and dissolve the yeast. Foam should begin to develop within 3 to 5 minutes.

Place the flour in a large bowl. Mix in the salt. Add the olive oil and yeast mixture. Stir well to combine ingredients until the dough has formed.

Remove the dough and knead by hand on a flour covered surface for about 10 minutes. Coat your hands with flour to keep the dough from clinging to your fingers. Add additional flour as necessary until the dough is no longer tacky and becomes smooth and elastic. Coat the inside of a large bowl with olive oil and roll the ball of dough against the surface to coat with oil as well. Cover and let the dough sit in a warm location until it doubles in size (30 to 60 minutes depending on the type of yeast). Once it has risen punch it down, press out all air bubbles and reform into another ball. Divide the ball into four sections, each of which will become a pizza portion. For calzone divide each of these sections into two parts to create a total of eight smaller balls.

Pizza dough can be frozen by tightly enclosing it in plastic wrap. Use within three to four weeks. Defrost at room temperature for about 3 - 4 hours or defrost in the refrigerator for a day. Be certain to keep the dough in the plastic. Exposed dough will get hard after prolonged exposure to air.

For Pizza, shape the dough by pressing and stretching with your hands or flatten with a rolling pin until it is about $^1/_8$ inch thick. Press up a slight berm around the rim to contain the fillings.

For calzone, roll the dough into uniform six inch wheels but eliminate the berm since the dough will be folded over and sealed along the edges.

Pre-heat the oven to 475 degrees for both pizza and calzone applications. Place the prepared pizza or calzone in the oven on a lightly oiled wire mesh pizza screen so that the crust is heated evenly during the cooking. Cook for 8 to 9 minutes depending on the thickness of the crust and the number of fillings. When done the edge of the crust or the outside of the calzone should be a uniform light tan. NOTE: pizza ingredients sometimes run and calzone can open during cooking and liquid will spill out. To prevent a dirty oven place a sheet of aluminum foil on the lower oven rack.

SHRIMP/AVOCADO CALZONE

  1 recipe for pizza dough (above)
     Olive oil
12 medium shrimp sliced into $^1/_2$ inch chunks
  3 chopped ripe Roma tomatoes
  1 sliced ripe avocado
  2 seeded and chopped Jalapeño peppers (optional)
     Freshly grated Parmesan cheese

Heat oven to 475 degrees

Take a 2 $^1/_2$ inch diameter ball of the prepared dough and roll into a relatively thin six inch circle. Drizzle a bit of olive oil on one half of the dough and layer on a tablespoon of chopped shrimp, a tablespoon of chopped tomato, a slice of avocado, and if you like, a teaspoon of chopped Jalapeño. Sprinkle on a bit of grated Parmesan cheese . Fold the dough over creating a triangular packet, or turnover, and press the edges together with the tines of a fork to seal. Pierce the top in one or two places with a knife point. Place on a pizza screen and bake for 8 - 10 minutes until a uniform golden brown color. Remove from the oven and serve either hot or cold.

Makes 6 calzone

SCALLOP/GARLIC CALZONE

This makes a delicate but filling calzone. The ricotta cheese is mild and compliments the flavor of the scallops and lemon juice. When cooked the garlic loses the strong raw garlic flavor.

  1 recipe for pizza dough (above)
     Olive oil
  6 large cloves garlic, each sliced thinly into six pieces
  4 sea scallops cut in eighths or 12 halved bay scallops
     Fresh lemon juice
  1 cup ricotta cheese
     Lightly chopped fresh parsley
     Salt and pepper to taste

Heat oven to 475 degrees

Take a 2 $^1/_2$ inch diameter ball of the prepared dough and roll into a relatively thin six inch circle. Drizzle a bit of the olive oil on one half of the dough. Lay out six garlic slices directly on the dough so that they will receive the greatest amount of heat. Add a tablespoon of the sea scallop pieces and squeeze on a few drops of lemon juice. Dot on the ricotta cheese. Place a few pieces of parsley on top, sprinkle with salt and pepper, fold over the dough and seal the edges by pressing with with the tines of a fork. Pierce the top in two places with the point of a knife. Bake in a 475 degree oven for 8 - 10 minutes or until crust is golden brown. Remove from oven and serve.

Makes 6 calzone   **(Calzone   continued   on   next   page)**

Other calzone fillings can include any fresh seafood, anchovies, marinated artichoke hearts, capers, chopped black olives, cilantro, Mexican salsa, sautéed onion and garlic, cooked spinach, mushrooms, feta and other cheeses.

MIXED SEAFOOD PIZZA

   1 **recipe for pizza dough (Pg. 145)**
   4 **sea scallops cut into quarters or 8 halved bay scallops**
   6 **mussels or clams steamed open and removed from shell**
   6 **shelled medium shrimp**
   2 **tablespoons olive oil (divided use)**
 $^{1}/_{2}$ **teaspoon fresh lemon juice**
   5 **thinly sliced Roma tomatoes**
   4 **sliced large mushrooms**
   3 **finely chopped cloves garlic**
   1 **cup grated mozzarella cheese**
      Salt and pepper to taste
      Chopped parsley or cilantro for garnish

Heat the oven to 475 degrees.

Prepare the dough as directed in the basic recipe and roll out into a 10 inch circle with raised berm around the edges. Brush or sprinkle on a light coating of olive oil.

Place the seafood in a small bowl with about a tablespoon of olive oil and a half teaspoon of lemon juice and coat all sides.

Distribute the tomato and mushroom slices around the dough interspersed with the seafood. Top with the chopped garlic and mozzarella cheese. Salt and pepper as desired.

Place the pizza on a wire pizza screen and transfer to the pre-heated oven. Bake for 8 to 9 minutes until cheese is melted and pie crust is golden tan. Slice into 6 pie-shaped pieces and garnish with parsley or cilantro according to your taste.

Other pizza options include pre-cooked octopus; blanched, sliced calamari; and anchovies (if using anchovies reduce the salt during the preparation.)

Makes 1 pizza for 2

SHRIMP PIZZA

         1 recipe for pizza dough (above)
         2 tablespoons olive oil (divided use)
        12 shelled medium shrimp
         6 strips of pimientoed red bell pepper (Pg. 156)
            Juice $^1/_2$ lemon
         3 thinly sliced cloves garlic
         4 thinly sliced Roma tomatoes
         6 black olives cut in half
    1 $^1/_2$ teaspoons dried dill weed
      $^1/_2$ cup tomato sauce mixed with 1 teaspoon sugar
      $^1/_2$ cup grated Cheddar cheese

Pre-heat the oven to 475 degrees.

Prepare the dough as directed in the basic recipe and roll out into a 10 inch circle with raised berm around the edges. Brush or sprinkle on a light coating of olive oil. Coat the shrimp and bell pepper strips in a mixture of olive oil and lemon juice. Distribute the tomato slices across the dough to cover. Lay on the uncooked shrimp in an orderly pattern and intersperse with black olives and strips of pimiento. Distribute the dill weed over the ingredients. Pour on the tomato sauce and cover with the grated Cheddar. Bake in the pre-heated oven for 8 - 10 minutes or until the crust is golden and the cheese is melted. Slice into 6 pie-shaped pieces and serve.

Makes 1 pizza for 2

MUSSEL/SHRIMP PIZZA

         1 recipe for pizza dough (above)
         1 tablespoon olive oil
         6 peeled medium shrimp
            Meat from 6 cooked medium mussels
         1 link precooked Italian sausage cut into $^1/_4$ inch disks
         3 finely chopped cloves garlic
      $^1/_2$ cup grated mozzarella cheese
      $^1/_2$ cup tomato sauce mixed with 1 teaspoon sugar
         6 fresh basil leaves

Pre-heat the oven to 475 degrees.

Prepare the dough and roll out into a 10 inch circle with raised edges. Brush on a light coating of olive oil. Alternate the shrimp and mussel meats around the pizza dough in an interesting pattern. Intersperse with the sausage disks and sprinkle on the chopped garlic. Distribute the cheese over the other ingredients. Pour on the tomato sauce and strategically place the basil leaves around the center. Bake in the pre-heated oven for 8 - 10 minutes until the crust is golden and the cheese is melted. Slice into six pie shaped pieces and serve.

SAUCES, DIPS AND MARINADES

RECIPES IN THIS CHAPTER

Sauces, dips and marinades have evolved to help us vary the flavor of the foods we eat. They are a valuable addition to cooking, and can add excitement to even bland foods. The trick is to make them so that they compliment the food rather than overwhelm it. In some cases this can be a close call, as in curry dishes where the curry flavor should be added in moderate degrees depending on the seafood used. There are also ethnic and regional variations such as Cajon, Southwestern and some Asian dishes where more spices are the rule rather than the exception. Fortunately, within these parameters there are many variables which can go into a sauce, so the chef is left with an endless number of options in their preparation. The sauces listed below are but a small sampling of what can be made. Almost all of these sauces can be varied by simply altering one or more ingredients. This is why sauce making can be so interesting for the chef. Experiment, taste, alter until you have made a basic sauce which reflects your own tastes. That is the test of a great sauce maker.

AIOLI SAUCE

This is a garlic based mayonnaise-type sauce. Properly made it has a smooth garlic flavor and makes an excellent dip or sauce for shrimp or calamari strips as well as other cooked sea foods. Easy to make.

- 1　egg yolk
- 5　pressed garlic cloves
- 1　tablespoon lemon juice
- 1　teaspoon white vinegar
- $^{1}/_{2}$　teaspoon salt
- 1　cup olive oil

Mix the egg yolk, the pressed garlic cloves, lemon juice, vinegar and salt with $^{1}/_{3}$ cup of olive oil. Beat strongly to blend, then gradually add the remaining oil, beating rapidly until thickened. You can make this sauce in advance and refrigerate until needed.

AVOCADO/CREAM SAUCE

- 1　ripe avocado
- 1　teaspoon lemon or lime juice
- $^{1}/_{2}$　cup half-and-half or sour cream
- 　　Salt and ground white pepper

Remove the pulp from the avocado and mash thoroughly with the citrus juice. Beat in the half-and-half or sour cream until the mixture is smooth. Salt and pepper to taste. Serve over any delicately flavored seafood. **Makes about 1 $^{1}/_{4}$ cups. As an additional note, you can force an avocado to ripen by placing it in a brown paper bag and putting it on a shelf outside the refrigerator. It will ripen in a few days.**

BASIC WHITE SAUCE

- 2 tablespoons butter
- 2 tablespoons flour
- 1 cup milk or half-and-half
  Salt to taste
  Dash of nutmeg

Melt the butter in a sauce pan and gradually stir in the flour. Slowly add the milk, stirring with a wire whisk or fork over low heat until homogenous and the sauce begins to thicken. Add a bit of salt and the nutmeg for flavor. This basic sauce can be lightened and made into a clam sauce by cutting the milk input in half and adding a half cup of clam juice. Replace the nutmeg with $^1/_2$ teaspoon of thyme and add the meat from one (6 $^1/_2$ ounce) can of minced or chopped clams.

BUTTERMILK / SOUR CREAM SAUCE

- $^1/_4$ cup cultured low fat buttermilk
- $^1/_4$ cup sour cream
- 1 beaten egg yolk
- 2 tablespoons lemon juice
- 1 teaspoon white vinegar
- 1 tablespoon finely chopped parsley
- $^1/_2$ teaspoon salt

Combine all the ingredients and whisk to mix thoroughly. Serve over seafood or pasta salads. By adding 1 tablespoon of lemon zest you can convert this into a fine lemon sauce.

CAPER SAUCE

- 3 tablespoons butter (divided use)
- 1 tablespoon flour
- 1 egg yolk
- $^1/_2$ teaspoon salt
- $^1/_2$ cup water
- 1 cup low-fat milk
- 2 tablespoons chopped capers
- 1 teaspoon caper juice
- $^1/_2$ teaspoon dried dill weed
- 2 teaspoons cream sherry

In a sauce pan melt two tablespoons butter and blend in the flour. Mix the egg yolk, salt, water and low fat milk and add to the flour/butter mixture. Bring close to boiling over medium-low heat. Stir constantly to prevent scorching. Add the remaining butter, capers, caper juice and dill weed. Stir until mixed and heat to simmer. Mix in sherry. Serve with fish, calamari, scallops and other seafoods.

CURRY SAUCE

> 2 tablespoons butter or olive oil
> 2 tablespoons flour
> 1 cup half-and-half
> $^1/_2$ teaspoon salt
> 2 to 4 teaspoons curry powder depending on your tolerance

Melt the butter and blend in the flour. Add the half-and-half slowly while stirring. Add salt and curry powder. Mix well and heat until thickened. Do not boil. You can make this into a curry/lime sauce by adding a half teaspoon of lime zest and 1 tablespoon of freshly squeezed lime juice.

CURRY / SOUR CREAM SAUCE

> 1 cup sour cream
> 2 tablespoons curry powder

Blend the curry powder into the sour cream, then heat the mixture before serving. You can vary the intensity of this sauce by adding more or less curry powder.

CRAB BOIL SPICES FOR SEAFOOD

This combination of spices imparts a distinct flavor to the boiled shellfish without overpowering.

> $^1/_2$ teaspoon mustard seed
> $^1/_2$ teaspoon coriander seed
> $^1/_2$ teaspoon whole cloves
> $^1/_2$ teaspoon black peppercorns
> 1 crumbled Bay leaf
> $^1/_4$ teaspoon cayenne pepper
> $^1/_2$ lemon in two pieces
> 1 tablespoon salt
> Live crabs or crayfish or shrimp in the shell

Mix the dry ingredients and tie into a square piece of thin cloth. Place the bag of spices and the lemon into 2 or 3 quarts of water and bring to a boil. Add the shellfish and return to a boil. Turn down the heat to a simmer and boil crabs for 10 to 15 minutes, crayfish and shrimp for 5 minutes.

FISH SAUCE

Fish sauce is also called anchovy sauce, noùc màm (sounds like nuke mom) (Vietnamese) or patis (Filipino). You can obtain this sauce in Asiatic food markets. It is made by fermenting fish in heavily salted water and then extracting and bottling the liquid. Some of the best comes from the Vietnamese island of Phù Quoc off the south coast. There was a small airfield serving a U.S. Navy coastal patrol detachment near the tiny town of An Thoi where I used to fly in mail and small supplies. This town was an authentic version of a Hollywood South Sea island set. Coconut palms swung out over the beach, fat hogs lay in the street and workmen in sarongs built small fishing boats and shaped the wood with adzes. There was also a pervasive smell of fermenting fish. The natives villagers made noùc màm. The fish was processed in huge vats made of vertical planks held together with twisted strips of slit bamboo. The fish went in the top, with water and salt, and the extract was tapped off at the bottom and bottled. It sounds strong, but used in moderation it makes a great addition to certain foods. Look on the next bottle of Lea & Perrins Worcestershire sauce and you will see anchovies listed as one of the ingredients, but because it is liquefied it is really the fish sauce that the Worcestershire makers use.

GUACAMOLE DIP

There are probably as many guacamole recipes as there are people who make this dip, but this mix works very well for me and always elicits favorable reactions from my guests.

    1 **ripe avocado**
       Juice of half lemon or lime
    2 **tablespoons grated onion**
       Dash Tabasco
       Dash Worcestershire sauce
       Sprinkle of garlic powder
    5 **chopped sprigs cilantro**
       Salt and pepper
    6 **peeled and cooked medium shrimp**

Remove and mash the avocado pulp in a bowl using a fork or potato masher. Add the citrus juice, grated onion, Tabasco, Worcestershire, garlic powder, and cilantro. Add salt and pepper to taste. The addition of shrimp adds another appealing dimension as well as a bit of complementary color. Finely chop four cooked shrimp and add to the other ingredients and mix well.

Concerning guacamole - try not to overpower the avocado flavor. This dish is best if prepared ahead and placed in the refrigerator for a few hours to blend the flavors.

HORSERADISH/SOUR CREAM SAUCE

    3 **tablespoons prepared horseradish**
    1 **cup sour cream**
    1 **teaspoon lemon or lime juice**
  1 ½ **teaspoons sugar**
       Sprinkle of salt

Mix well and serve over your favorite seafood or use as a dip for deep fried seafood.

LEMON / BUTTER SAUCE

Add the juice of one lemon to ¼ pound melted butter (1 stick). Serve over seafood.

LOUISIANA BROWN ROUX

A roux is nothing but a flour-oil mixture which is used as a thickening agent, especially in Cajon cooking. Depending on preparation time a roux can be white, tan or brown. The brown roux is a necessary ingredient in certain Cajon dishes, especially Gumbo (pg. 137), but it can be used as a base for other brown sauces and gravies by the addition of other ingredients. Making the brown roux is a time consuming business. If you are going to begin cooking Cajon, make a large amount and then either refrigerate or freeze what you don't use. The roux will keep for many weeks in the refrigerator or months in the freezer. If it settles out into its constituent parts during storage simply recombine with a wire whisk before using.

For a Louisiana brown roux

> **One cup general purpose flour**
> **One cup vegetable oil**

Mix the two ingredients in a skillet over low heat with a large wooden spoon and then continue stirring until the mixture turns a golden brown and gives off a rich nutty smell. This can take up to an hour. Take your time and keep the heat low to prevent scorching. Once the mixture is browned remove from heat, cool and either use or store.

MAYONNAISE / DILL SAUCE

This is a great dipping sauce for deep fried sea food.

$^1/_4$ **cup mayonnaise**
$1 ^1/_2$ **teaspoons lemon juice**
$^1/_2$ **teaspoon dry dill weed**

Thoroughly mix all the ingredients and let stand for at least one hour in the refrigerator. You can substitute Ranch dressing for the mayonnaise to make an interesting alternative sauce.

MEXICAN SALSA

If you live in an area where there are a large number of Mexican restaurants, you will know that there are an infinite variety of Mexican salsas available. The recipe that follows can be changed in many ways to suit the taste of the maker.

3   **seeded and chopped jalapeño peppers**
2   **large chopped tomatoes**
1   **eight ounce can tomato sauce**
$^1/_2$ **white onion - chopped**
2   **large finely diced cloves garlic**
$^1/_2$ **cup chopped cilantro**
2   **teaspoons cider vinegar**

1 teaspoon coarse black pepper
2 teaspoons sugar
1 teaspoon salt

Mix all the ingredients. Place in blender for a short period to reduce larger chunks. Allow the mixture to sit in the refrigerator overnight to combine the flavors.

MEXICAN SOUR CREAM SAUCE

1 cup sour cream
2 pressed cloves garlic
2 tablespoons chopped cilantro
2 tablespoons seeded, finely chopped mild green chili peppers (Anaheim)
$^1/_2$ teaspoon salt

Mix ingredients well and let stand in the refrigerator overnight to blend. Serve over seafood enchiladas and similar Mexican dishes.

NEWBURG SAUCE

4 tablespoons butter
2 tablespoons flour
1 cup half-and-half
2 beaten egg yolks
1 teaspoon paprika
Dash cayenne pepper
$^1/_2$ teaspoon salt
2 tablespoons sherry

Melt the butter and blend in the flour. Stir in the half-and-half and bring to a simmer. Add a bit of the heated sauce to the egg yolks, stir and add to the flour/butter mix. Sprinkle on the paprika, cayenne and salt. Finally, stir in the sherry and serve over seafood. This sauce can be made ahead and reheated.

OLIVE / ANCHOVY SAUCE

10 finely chopped pitted green or black olives
1 (2 ounce) can anchovies, drained and finely chopped
2 finely chopped cloves garlic
1 tablespoon olive oil
1 tablespoon lemon juice
Pepper to taste

Combine the olives, anchovies and garlic. Dribble on olive oil and lemon juice and mix well. Use as a sauce over stuffed squid or fish fillets or by itself on toast or crackers.

PARSLEY PESTO

It is my habit to make up a large fresh batch of parsley pesto when my garden yields its first good annual crop. It is one more indicator of the passage of time and becomes a pseudo holy event.

- **1 bunch parsley**
- **2 pressed cloves garlic**
- **1 tablespoon dried basil leaves**
- **2 tablespoons olive oil**
  Salt and pepper to taste.
- **2 tablespoons freshly grated Parmesan cheese**

Roughly chop the parsley. Combine the pressed garlic with the basil and olive oil and add to the parsley. Sprinkle on the salt and pepper then grate on the Parmesan cheese. Mix well and let sit overnight. Serve as a dressing with seafood or by itself on crackers. You can add finely chopped avocado or finely chopped marinated artichoke heart to alter the flavor.

PIMIENTOED SWEET RED PEPPER

1 or 2 sweet red peppers

Cook the red pepper(s) under the broiler or on the grill until the skin begins to blister and turn black. Turn often during the process for even cooking. Remove the pepper(s) to a bowl and cover with plastic wrap to steam. After the pepper(s) cool peel off the easily removed skin and remove the seeds. The meat can then be cut into smaller pieces for use and stored in a jar of olive oil with cut up garlic cloves. Lasts about a week in the refrigerator.

Aside from its use in and on cooked dishes pimientos make a great sandwich spread with cream cheese.

RÉMOULADE SAUCE

Rémoulade sauce is a different and wonderful cold sauce with a mustard flavor. It is served over a variety of dishes, but it is especially good over cooked fish and shell fish.

- **$^1/_2$ cup mayonnaise**
- **1 tablespoon Dijon type mustard**
- **2 tablespoons tarragon vinegar**
- **2 finely chopped green onions**
- **2 finely chopped cloves garlic**
- **1 tablespoon finely chopped parsley**
- **4 teaspoons fish sauce (Pg. 152) - (or)**
- **3 finely chopped anchovies**
- **1 tablespoon chopped capers**

Mix the ingredients together and let stand in the refrigerator for three hours to blend the flavors.

SATÉ SAUCE

This Indonesian peanut sauce can be purchased in most Asian food markets, but it is easy enough to make using ingredients found in most homes. Don't skimp on the cayenne or curry. Indonesians like "hot" sauces.

- **1 tablespoon creamy peanut butter**
- **1 tablespoon canola oil**
- **1 $^1/_2$ teaspoons soy sauce**
- **2 teaspoons curry powder**
- **2 tablespoons finely chopped green onion - green part**
- **2 pressed cloves garlic**
- **$^1/_2$ teaspoon sugar**
- **$^1/_2$ teaspoon cayenne pepper**

Combine all the ingredients and use as a marinade or as a dipping sauce for meat and seafood.

SEAFOOD COCKTAIL SAUCE

- **$^1/_2$ cup ketchup**
- **2 tablespoons prepared horseradish**
- **Juice $^1/_2$ lemon or lime**
- **$^1/_2$ teaspoon Worcestershire sauce (optional)**

Mix ingredients together and use on raw clams, oysters, etc. Some cooks like to add a dash of Worcestershire sauce as well.

SOUR CREAM AND DILL SAUCE

- **2 tablespoons butter**
- **2 teaspoons flour**
- **$^1/_2$ cup sour cream**
- **$^1/_4$ cup half-and-half**
- **1 teaspoon dried dill weed**
- **$^1/_2$ teaspoon salt**

Melt the butter and blend in the flour. Add the sour cream, half-and-half, dill and salt. Heat over a low flame until the mixture begins to thicken slightly. Remove from the heat and serve.

To make this into a sour cream/dill/caper sauce add in a tablespoon of finely chopped capers.

SWEET AND SOUR SAUCE

$^1/_4$ cup water
  2 tablespoons sugar
  2 tablespoons red wine vinegar
  2 tablespoons soy sauce
  1 (8 ounce) can tomato sauce
$^1/_2$ cup finely diced onion
  1 tablespoon cornstarch
  2 tablespoons cream sherry

Combine the water, sugar, vinegar and soy sauce in small sauce pan and heat to boiling. Add the tomato sauce and onion. Return to a boil then reduce heat and simmer for 5 minutes.

Blend the cornstarch into the two tablespoons of sherry. Stir into the sauce. Again heat to boiling and continue stirring until the sauce is thickened and translucent.

TARTAR SAUCE

  1 cup of mayonnaise
  2 tablespoons finely chopped green onion - green part
  1 tablespoon finely chopped parsley
  2 teaspoons lemon juice
  2 teaspoons white vinegar
  2 tablespoons finely chopped sweet or dill pickle (cook's choice)
$^1/_2$ teaspoon dry mustard
  1 teaspoon sugar

Mix the ingredients well and and let stand in the refrigerator for 3 hours to blend.

TERIYAKI SAUCE AND MARINADE

  2 tablespoons soy sauce
  1 tablespoon Japanese mirin or cream sherry
  1 tablespoon water
  2 teaspoons sugar

Mix the ingredients and stir until the sugar is dissolved. Use as a marinade or as a sauce during cooking.

Shellfish eaters are a fortunate group. Shellfish are generally low in fat and saturated fat, but high in protein, iron and zinc. Shellfish are low in sodium but contribute iodine and certain of the B vitamins to the diet. Most are not high in cholesterol averaging 50 to 70mg per 3.5 ounce serving. Calamari, shrimp, crawfish and sea urchin roe are the cholesterol exceptions, but eaten in moderation even these can be enjoyed periodically for their other benefits.

Please note that the following figures should only be used as a rough guide since the values can vary depending on where the catch was taken and on other factors such as water temperature, the season of the year, the species and local water nutrients.

100 grams(3.5 oz.) edible portion	calories	protein grams	fat grams	sodium mgs	cholesterol mgs
Abalone(fried)	188	19.4	6.8	586	93
Calamari(squid)(fried)	174	17.8	7.5	303	258
Clams (steamed)	155	26.8	2.1	118	70
Crab (Blue-steamed)	101	20.1	1.7	276	99
Crayfish (steamed)	113	23.7	1.4	68	176
Lobster(steamed)	97	20.2	.6	377	71
Mussel(steamed)	170	24.0	4.4	366	56
Octopus(raw)	82	15.0	1.0	228	48
Oysters (raw)	68	6.9	2.5	110	54
Scallops (raw)	87	16.7	.8	160	33
Sea Urchin Roe (raw)	139	22.2	6.4	90	371
Shrimp (steamed)	98	20.7	1.0	221	194
Whelk (boiled)	273	47.2	.8	408	129

THE JAPANESE ART OF GYOTAKU OR NATURE PRINTING

The Japanese art of nature printing, or Gyotaku, dates back over 170 years. The process was originally used to record the catches of sports fish, but it was not long before the Japanese recognized that the prints were a distinct art form worthy of mounting and signing.

The readers of this book will notice that the majority of the introductory chapter prints depict objects and creatures other than fish. The author began experimenting with and printing soft-bodied creatures, like squid and octopus, more than 10 years ago. He also taught himself how to make attractive prints from the exo-skeletons of crustaceans and the shells of mollusks.

In Japan the signature block consists of a "chop" which is printed directly on some portion of the print. The chop essentially becomes a part of the overall composition and its placement is carefully selected. The author's chop translates into "Sea Eagle" to commemorate his 24 years as a Navy flier.

BASIC TECHNIQUE FOR FISH PRINTING

To "print" a fish you must first rid it of mucus, carefully dry the surface, as well as the inside of the mouth and under the gills and fins. You then apply paint or ink to the fish, but avoid putting paint on the eye or eye socket. Once the paint has been applied, lightly dampened rice paper or tightly woven fabric is rubbed or pressed on to make the impression. Since no color was applied to the eye you now use your talents as an artist to record these. This is the only place where hand painting is permitted. This printing technique is not as easy as it sounds, but if properly done the results can be both realistic and striking.

The author uses watercolor for his fish prints because the edges blend readily where adjacent colors meet, but watercolor is not successful when used on crustaceans and mollusks. The shells of shrimp, crab and lobsters do not lend themselves to smooth watercolor application and watercolor tends to leach into the calcium-based mollusk shells producing generally poor results. Acrylic paints are a better choice for these alternative types of prints. Acrylics can be applied more thickly than watercolors and do not run so easily. Acrylics also clean easily between impressions because of their water base. With all water based pigments the sea food can be consumed after the prints have been made.

Don Hubbard has been working with this art form for over twenty years after seeing an excellent Japanese example in the library of the Scripp's Institution of Oceanography in 1968. Since that time he has produced well over a thousand nature prints using fish and shells and has pioneered in printing crustaceans and the soft-bodied creatures mentioned above.

161

He is a long-time member of the Nature Printing Society, a nation-wide organization devoted to this unique art. For information about joining the Nature Printing Society please write to Sonja Larsen, 7675 Interlachen Road, Lake Shore, MN 56468-8650

Also note that silhouette copies of fish and shellfish can be made using blueprint paper or cloth. To obtain blueprint materials suitable for this technique please contact Blueprint-Printables, 1400 A. Marsten Rd., Burlingame, CA 94010 1 800/356 0445

Further information about nature printing can be obtained on the internet by using the keyword, "gyotaku"

Framed and matted copies of the prints in this book and others are available from Sea Eagle Publications. For size and pricing of these prints and others please request a catalog from the company at P.O. Box 180550, Coronado, CA 92178.

INDEX